D. J. SMITH

Discovering
Horse-drawn
Farm Machinery

SHIRE PUBLICATIONS LTD

Contents

Cover photograph by Cadbury Lamb: An International Deering self-delivery reaper from Alscott Farm Museum, North Devon, being demonstrated at Wroughton, Swindon, during a Science Museum Open Day.

Printed in Great Britain by C. I. Thomas & Sons (Haverfordwest) Ltd, Press Buildings, Merlins Bridge, Haverfordwest.

Introduction

Until the period of the First World War most of the machines and vehicles used in farming were dragged by horses. Although oxen had been widely used from even earlier periods they had been gradually phased out and replaced by horses in the same way that horses were made redundant by the internal combustion engine. The breeds of heavy draught horse, mainly used in agriculture, were greatly improved and increased in numbers during the eighteenth century, which was a period of revolutions in both agriculture and industry. Between the reign of Queen Anne and the Napoleonic Wars a whole new range of drills, ploughs, cultivators and harvesting machines came into being, few of which would have worked successfully without the horse as motive power. The horse provided not only strength but greater activity and quicker response than other beasts of burden.

This book is mainly concerned with types of implement and machine used on the average British farm from the period of agricultural improvements during the eighteenth century to the 1930s. Some less progressive farms were still using horse-drawn implements well into the 1950s, although two world wars and the need to 'speed the plough' greatly reduced the horse population on most farms and holdings. It is unlikely that this could ever be changed although there are still some jobs on farms, especially hill farms, market gardens and smallholdings, for which the horse is more economical than the tractor, particularly as a result of the ever increasing cost and scarcity of imported fuels. On dangerous slopes, small plots and between orchard trees the single horse is often a far better proposition than four wheels.

ACKNOWLEDGEMENTS

The author wishes to thank the following for their help in compiling this book: the curator and staff of the Museum of English Rural Life; the curator and staff of the Staffordshire County Museum; the curator and staff of the Hereford and Worcester County Museum; B. B. Murdock, Esq; C. A. Jewell, Esq; Miss C. Purser. Photographs are acknowledged as follows: the HDV Series, plate 27; Museum of English Rural Life, University of Reading, plates 1, 2, 4, 6, 8, 9, 13, 14, 18, 20, 21, 23, 29; Pitstone Local History Society, plates 19, 22, 30; Crown Copyright, Science Museum, London, plates 5, 7, 11, 16, 17; photo, Science Museum, plates 10, 12, 24; lent to Science Museum by Ransomes, Sims & Jefferies Ltd, plate 25; lent to Science Museum by Royal Scottish Museum, plate 3; D. J. Smith, plates 15, 28, 31 (photographs by P. Treherne) and 26.

1. The plough

The plough is the basic and most widely used of all farm implements; it was preceded only by the pick-like digging stick and possibly by attempts at scratching the surface of light soils with a branch or bush. The obvious function of the plough was to improve on the digging stick, working on a larger scale with a more efficient routine. In order that the land might produce good crops it had to be broken up, turned and weathered. To this end the plough inverts furrows, exposing them to the cleansing and disintegrating effect of air, rain, frost and snow. The first plough in history was an enlarged and refined version of the digging stick, consisting of a triangular structure of wooden members, the lower part — in contact with the ground — being of fire-hardened wood but later tipped with a flint or piece of iron. While the forward-upper extension could be fitted to the neck yoke of a pair of oxen, the opposite end was a single handle for guiding the plough and keeping it steady. The earliest known ploughs were used by the ancient Egyptians, although perhaps the Chinese used them even earlier, long before 1500 BC. The Egyptians may first have used either the horn of an ox or a pointed flintstone for the digging end, before adopting the metal tip. The handle remained single for many centuries, being held in both hands and used for pushing, to assist the team, almost as much as for guiding. The first ploughs broke and stirred the surface of the soil but were unable to lay a regular furrow in the modern sense.

Fig. 1. Ancestors of the modern plough. A, B: digging sticks. C: early Egyptian ox plough. D: breast plough.

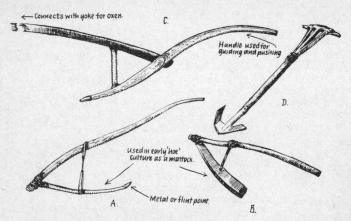

← Connects with yoke for oxen.

C.

Handle used for guiding and pushing

D.

Used in early 'hoe' culture as a mattock.

Metal or flint point.

A.

B.

Fig. 2. Early cultivation. Left: early Egyptian ox plough. Right: digging
stick.

There are numerous references to ploughs in early literature
from the Old Testament to Virgil's *Georgics*. A primitive version
of the share and coulter was introduced by the natives of Cisalpine
Gaul, while the ancient Greeks were the first to use wheeled
ploughs. The Romans made much use of ploughs but did not
introduce them to Britain, where a primitive Celtic plough was
found to be in use at the time of their first invasion. The ancient
Britons and other Celtic peoples preferred small square fields to
strip-farming methods.

The Saxon and medieval ploughs used in Britain for over six
centuries were awkward and cumbersome, showing very little
advance on types used by the Greeks and Romans. On heavy soil
they needed a team of eight or ten oxen with men and women
following the plough to break up the larger clods with mattocks.
This was part of the strip-farming system popular in most parts of
western Europe during the middle ages. The plough team was
frequently owned and shared by a village community. The length
of each depression or furrow was the length of a strip, known as a
furlong (220 yards or 200 metres), later used as a measure of
distance. Owing to the scarcity of iron only the digging parts of the
share and coulter were metallic, at least until the eighteenth
century when iron production greatly increased.

Fig. 3. Saxon plough.

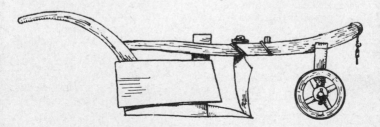

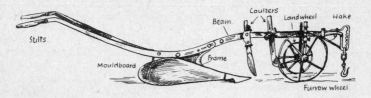

Fig. 4. Newcastle plough.

Early improvements

The later use of a mouldboard assisted in the proper turning of furrows. It was made of hardened wood, later sheathed with iron. While a type of mouldboard was used in medieval times it was not brought to workable perfection until the seventeenth century. One of the great innovators of this period was Walter Blith or Blithe, who wrote a treatise on the theory of the plough. Blith lived and worked during the English Civil Wars, not only improving on the older types but describing their regional variations. Only those parts of the plough in direct contact with the soil were iron and some superstitious farmers, right up to the mid nineteenth century, considered that too much iron might poison the land. By the mid seventeenth century there were many varieties of plough, especially in the design of the share, and there was much controversy about their use and general purpose. Usually the share for hard and stony ground was well pointed, but a much lighter, blunter and shorter share was used on light soils. Coulters or cutting knives could be straight or curved, placed either at the front or back of the share and sometimes in pairs or one behind the other. The normal position was for a single coulter to precede the share.

During the 1730s a plough with a much lighter framework and more curved mouldboard than hitherto was introduced from Holland. It was first adopted in Britain on a farm near Rotherham in South Yorkshire but was later used — with improvements — in all parts of the British Isles and was known as the Rotherham plough. Its main feature was an iron-plated mouldboard.

Later in the eighteenth century a Scot named James Small, farming in the Border country, introduced the so-called Berwickshire plough. This had handles and fittings of wrought iron and a share of cast iron. Although ideal for a short period, the share had to be constantly resharpened, and this was its main drawback. Small's plough was also known as the 'scientific plough' as he calculated the curves and positions of the main parts with great accuracy. The first successful plough with an all-iron frame was introduced by William Penny in 1800.

In 1803 Robert Ransome of East Anglia took out patents for a process of chilling and hardening iron parts in contact with the soil, especially the underside of the share. This was made self-sharpening through use and friction, requiring very little attention during its working life. Later during the nineteenth century both share and mouldboard were widely made of chilled steel.

Parts of the plough

The typical horse plough has several working parts and accessories. The main parts are the coulter, share and breast or mouldboard, without which the plough would be unable to function.

The coulter has several variations from a miniature ploughshare or wedge shape to a disc-like wheel and the more familiar knife blade. They are bolted on to the frame, which in turn is attached to the main body or beam of the plough. The coulter consists of a sharpened edge preceding the share and cutting into the soil to a considerable depth. The miniature share may be known as a skim coulter or jointer and is mainly used where there is a mass of old vegetation or stubble to bury, often before deep ploughing. The depth and angle of cut of a coulter is adjustable.

The mouldboard is fitted to a frame or body of steel, cast iron or wood. It turns the furrow slice to one side and is smooth and shiny

Fig. 5. Parts of a plough: 1: quadrant. 2, 2a: hakes. 3: drag weight, fitted to some coulters. 4: spanner or wynch. 5: mouldboard. 6, 6a, 6b, 6c, 6d: types of coulter. 7: frame coupling. 8: footing. 9: land or side cap. 10: beam. 11: share. 12: slade. 13: frame.

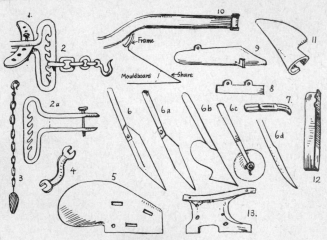

through constant friction. The share or point of the plough precedes the mouldboard and does much of the work of slicing. While the coulter cuts vertically the share slices horizontally. It improves the cut of the coulter but does not cover the full width of the furrow, allowing the adjacent mouldboard to make the final twist. It may be detached from the front or foot of the mouldboard when showing signs of wear.

An L-section steel or iron bar known as the slade runs along the bottom of the furrow, while a side or land cap may be fitted next to the unploughed land surface. Both of these are needed to steady the plough. The slade, bolted to the bottom of the frame, is sometimes known as the base of the plough, while the land cap keeps unploughed soil from falling into the furrow. Slade, land cap and mouldboard are fixed to a footing, frame coupling and breast coupling respectively. Most ploughs carry a small curved spanner, used for minor adjustments, on the offside handle. Some ploughs have an adjustable iron scraper to keep the share clean, fixed in a near vertical position.

The beam is the backbone of the plough; to it are attached the working parts and also the handles and draught connections. It may be of metal or wood, according to age or type, although from the second half of the nineteenth century most ploughs in daily use have been iron or steel throughout. Some wooden ploughs were made during the early twentieth century and may be seen at ploughing matches, a country pastime that has greatly revived since the Second World War.

The hake or clevis, at the front of the beam, is a notched loop of metal; it has a short draught chain, which is adjusted on the notches. By changing the position of the chain the plough digs more or less deeply into the ground. The chain is also useful in adjusting the draught gear in relation to the size and conformation of the plough horses or oxen used. Raising the chain and increasing the distance between draught animals and plough lowers the share. Grain crops need far less depth of ploughing than root crops. Although the hake is a vertical loop it moves laterally on a horizontal plane by means of a crescent-shaped quadrant. This allows the hake to be adjusted either to the left or right, giving the plough a tendency to move either to one side or the other as required.

The handles of the plough, often known as stilts, are attached in pairs at the rear of the beam, each pair converging to an apex on the beam. These are used by the ploughman as a means of control and balance. Some wooden ploughs had a single handle throughout the eighteenth century.

Most of the later horse ploughs had two wheels, these being of unequal size. They are fitted near the fore end of the beam, the larger wheel being in the furrow while the smaller or land wheel travels on the upper or unploughed surface. Wheels help to reduce friction and make draught easier for the team. They also help to control the height and width of the furrow. With a swing plough (one without wheels) greater strength has to be exercised by both ploughman and team than with other types.

Operation

In operation the coulter of a plough makes a deep perpendicular cut, which is thrown back as a furrow, then divided from its sole or former place of attachment by the share. The furrow slice is then inverted by the angle of the mouldboard, which has a hollow outward curve. Different types of share make different types of furrow, varying in width and shape. A high or crested furrow is created by the wing of the mouldboard being much higher than the share point. The rectangular or com-

Fig. 6. The plough in the furrow. A: field or land unploughed. B: headland for turning. C: newly turned furrows. D: furrow wheel. E: land wheel. F: coulter, making forward cut. G: share making sideways slice. H: slice about to be turned. I: mouldboard for turning furrow slice. J: furrow slice falling into place. K: stilts or plough handles.

Fig. 7. Digging or digger plough.

monplace furrow is made by a flat level-edged share which leaves broad flat furrow soles. The ideal form of ploughing, throughout the eighteenth and nineteenth centuries, was to make a furrow slice as even and unbroken as possible. For this a fairly long mouldboard was necessary, as seen in the match plough used for competitions and demonstrations. It laid the furrow at an angle of 45 degrees, which was considered the best for drainage and exposure on most types of land. The later digging or digger plough, with a much shorter mouldboard and greater curve of the board, had the effect of breaking up the furrow, turning it as a gardener might twist his spade in digging a small plot. This was considered better for medium to light soil but has long been a matter of controversy in farming circles. A field broken by a digger plough certainly has a more untidy and less pleasing appearance than one ploughed in the more conventional style.

Ploughed fields are divided into areas known as lands or sections, often marked out by the ploughman in advance of other work. These were areas divided by furrows, being of near equal width. On light soil and places of easy drainage a land was about 22 yards (20 metres) wide. On heavy ground, where the furrows served more as drains, the land was usually narrower, sometimes as little as 5 yards (4.5 metres) wide.

One-way ploughs

Important variations of the plough include several one-way types, of which the most interesting is the turnwrest. This can be either a wheeled plough or a swing plough, although the modern version may rely on a small single wheel in a central position under the fore end of the beam. The main advantage of the turnwrest is its ability to turn the furrow to either side without the body of the plough having to be turned, according to prior adjustment. All furrows are laid alternately left and right, all sloping in the same direction. The first turnwrest types used in Britain were known as Kent ploughs, widely used on the undulating downlands of Kent and Sussex, for which this type of work and implement was best suited. It may be traced back to the sixteenth century and perhaps earlier and was used by many Sussex farmers on the South Downs until the 1920s. Despised in some areas as heavy and cumbersome, these were just the features that contributed to its efficiency, a plough with plenty of weight proving essential for the chalk hills of the south-east. A great advantage of the turnwrest in hilly and undulating fields was that all furrows could be laid uphill, preventing the natural tendency for soil to work loose and fall away in a downhill direction. When set for throwing a furrow to the right, the so-called groundwrest and fixing peg or tool were transferred to the opposite side of the plough. This bore on the

Fig. 8. Kent turnwrest plough.

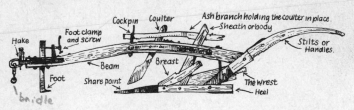

Fig. 9. Elevation of turnwrest (swing or foot) plough, late eighteenth century.

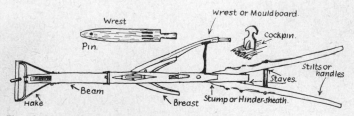

Fig. 10. Plan of turnwrest (swing or foot) plough.

11

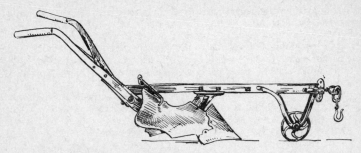

Fig. 11. Modern turnwrest plough, late nineteenth century.

coulter, which was further adjusted by pegs through slots. For throwing a furrow to the left the groundwrest was adjusted in reverse order. Turnwrest ploughs were considered ideal for temporary conversion to skim ploughs, especially for clearing stubble, this being done with the addition of a broadshare about 3½ inches (90 millimetres) wide and 20 inches (500 millimetres) long.

Fig. 12. Balance plough.

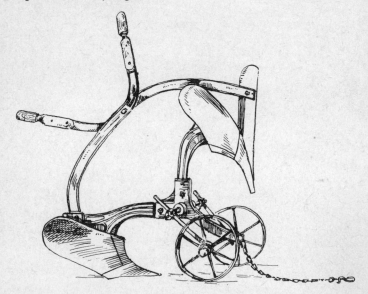

A later version of the one-way plough was known as the balance plough or 'cock-up', which had two shares on the same frame. These were mounted one above the other, the lower share being in contact with the soil while the other was carried to one side and much higher than ground level. They were made to revolve on a central beam, adjusted by handles at the rear. This was always a two-wheeled plough. Other, less complex one-way ploughs had a share and mouldboard that could be changed by swivelling when the beam was raised.

Multi-furrow ploughs

A double or multi-furrow plough was invented during the mid seventeenth century but required so many oxen or horses that turning at the headland, or end of each furrow, became a difficult manoeuvre. A more efficient multi-furrow plough was used in Staffordshire by a man named Pitt from 1796, but this seems to have been restricted to local use. Multi-furrow ploughs were little seen until a lighter and more compact version was introduced by the firm of Ransomes in 1873. Even this proved more successful in places such as the United States and Canada where fields or unfenced holdings were much larger than in Britain. The main advantage of the multi-furrow plough was in time saving although traditional farmers and ploughmen looked askance at such inventions, claiming that they were less under individual control than the single-furrow type and likely to lower the standards of a time-honoured craft.

Fig. 13. Riding or gang plough.

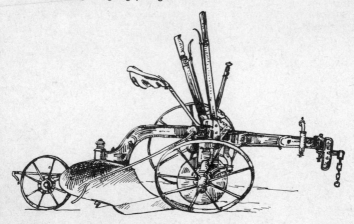

A version of the multi-furrow plough was the so-called riding plough or sulky, perfected in the United States of America and little used in Britain. Riding ploughs had a high sprung seat similar to that of a light two-wheeled cart used for showing and exercising trotting horses and also known as a sulky. (Having room for one person only, it was considered antisocial, so accounting for its name.) The seat was mounted above a solid steel frame on two large wheels and a smaller trailing wheel. Furrow wheels were of a dished appearance and fixed on inclined axles. The shares could be adjusted from the driving seat by means of hand levers. Coulters were in the form of disc wheels. A few multi-furrow ploughs were also walking ploughs while some riding ploughs had single shares. In Britain the multi-furrow plough came into its own with the advent of the tractor.

Disc plough

A disc or disk plough was sometimes used towards the end of the nineteenth century, although better adapted to tractor haulage than to animal draught. This again was either a riding or a walking machine, its main feature being the substitution of revolving convex discs in place of the normal share and mouldboard. Each disc, of which most ploughs had three, was mounted on an inclined axle at an angle to both horizontal and vertical planes. It cut deeply into the ground, revolving as it moved forward. An adjustable scraper on each disc prevented the machine from clogging, although it was not recommended for heavy or sticky ground. It was claimed to leave certain kinds of soil in a 'mellow, porous condition', at its best when the land to be ploughed was naturally dry or well drained.

Fig. 14. Multiple disc plough.

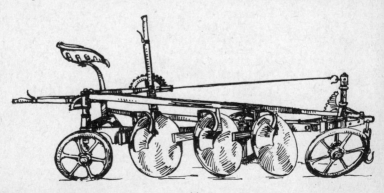

Specialised ploughs

Highly specialised ploughs were the ridging plough, the subsoil plough and the gripping plough, all of which were drawn by horses, at least until the Second World War. The ridging plough had double mouldboards, one on each side, terminating in a forward thrusting point, throwing up ridges in which to plant potatoes and other root crops. The subsoil plough was of conventional design with share and coulter but without the mouldboard. It followed behind an ordinary plough to strike an even deeper furrow, making the soil fully porous and easier for plant roots to grow in, where this was deemed necessary.

The gripping plough or drainage plough was used in making underground runnels, which began to replace open ditches or reliance on the furrows of ordinary ploughland during the second half of the eighteenth century. This led to the eventual use of enclosed clay pipes or land tiles, widely manufactured in Victorian England and still used on some farms in Yorkshire and the eastern counties to the present day. A so-called mole drainage plough of this type was invented by Cuthbert Clarke during the 1790s, although other, less efficient gripping ploughs appeared earlier in the century. They all had a variety of deep rods with a forward pointing arrowhead attachment that could penetrate soil up to a depth of 20 inches (500 millimetres), making horizontal underground passages for circular drains. Mud and water were removed from the drains by means of a hand scoop or drain lade.

Hundreds of different ploughs were invented at one time or another, although they were mainly variations of those already mentioned. Their use depended on many factors, including weather conditions, types of soil and local customs or prejudices. Nineteenth-century manufacturers, eager to please as many farmers as possible, advertised far more than they ever sold, if only to make a good impression. Standardisation was an idea little heard of then but only a bare minimum of the average range in the catalogue was ever stocked in large numbers. Certain types had to be made to order but this was willingly done at short notice.

Most of the ploughs mentioned in this chapter were drawn by horses, usually pairs working side by side. On heavy land teams of four or more may have been used, while the turnwrest plough of Kent and Sussex was drawn, in many cases, by three horses one behind the other. A small single-furrow plough, designed for use by smallholders or market gardeners, could be drawn by a pony or donkey. Some ploughs were even drawn by women.

2. Clod-breaking machines

Various types of equipment were used after ploughing to improve the tilth or area and depth of soil needed for cultivation. They may be classified as cultivators, grubbers, harrows and rollers. Some were known merely as clod crushers or presses and consisted of heavy ridged wheels on an iron or wooden framework drawn by a single horse between shafts. They followed the plough and were usually designed as a set of three or more wheels on a single axle, supported on the land side by a much lighter wheel than those in the furrow. Before their widespread use the ploughman or his assistants often carried large mallets or mattocks (sometimes known as beetles) with which to beat down or break up the larger clods.

One of the earliest cultivators, also known as a scuffler, was introduced during the 1820s by a Scottish farmer named Finlayson, although his design was more like the later grubber than the true cultivator. Similar to a harrow mounted on wheels, it was meant to serve as an intermediate machine between plough and harrow, stirring the soil deeply but not too rigorously, while bringing unwanted weeds and rubbish to the surface like a hoe does.

The grubber

This was a frame-type implement mounted on three wheels. Also known as the Scotch grubber from its resemblance to Finlayson's machine of the early 1820s, it was later improved by Scoular and others. Curved tines on the underside of the frame were adjusted by raising the whole structure (a triangular framework) by parallel vertical lift. While the rear wheels were on bell cranks, the forewheel was fixed under the frame by means of a stalk or extension bar screwed to a swivel collar just behind the

Fig. 15. Scotch grubber.

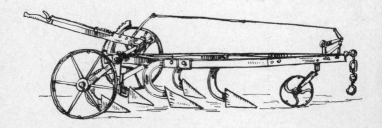

16

draw hook. Tines were either sprung or rigid, the latter being more popular in Britain, although spring tines were used more frequently in North America and continental Europe. There were three rows of tines, each row having plenty of space for clearance.

The great advantage claimed for the grubber was a better distribution of weight than with normal cultivators. In later types of cultivator the tines were well behind the main wheels so that the heavier soils caused a loss of balance, throwing too much weight on the front of the machine — both frame and wheels. The grubber was a walking rather than a riding machine, heavy and cumbersome to use, less popular on this account than its later counterparts. Unlike most cultivators it could not be used — with adjustments — as a drill, hoe or ridger, and so it was less versatile. The grubber was long and low, far less compact and easy to transport than the cultivator.

Cultivators

Perhaps the most popular cultivator was the English bar type, which closely resembled a multiple-horse hoe. Tines were fixed to special tine bars extending at right angles across the rear of the machine. These could be raised and lowered and the tines set at various depths. Tines were of bar steel, rectangular in section,

Fig. 16. A: bar cultivator (self-lift). B: spring tine cultivator.

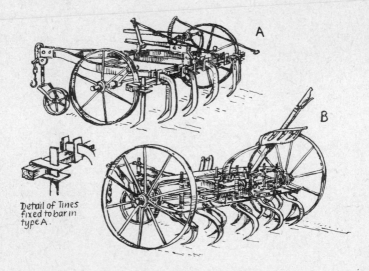

Detail of Tines fixed to bar in type A.

17

curving inwards at the points. There were two rows of tines with alternating long and short curves at their extremities. Adjustment of the tines could be made laterally along the bar for necessary clearances. The whole was mounted on three wheels with a small wheel at the front of the frame and two much larger wheels in front of the tine bars. The tine bars, being behind the main wheels, could work to a broader gauge than the grubber and other similar machines. This type could also be fitted with a triple ridging attachment. Working width was about 6 feet 2 inches (1.88 metres) and weight 5 hundredweights (254 kilograms).

The horse rake cultivator was another popular version of this type, invented by a man named Howard during the 1890s and sometimes known as Howard's Champion, a name under which it was advertised. It worked on much the same principle as the dump rake of the hayfield, having up to nine tines, usually sickle-shaped, attached to brackets on the axle, which could be raised and lowered by using a lever operated from the driving seat. This was a fairly swift riding machine, the quick lever action getting rid of weeds and rubbish with great efficiency. Pitch and depth of the tines had to be adjusted individually.

Martin's cultivator, also of the late nineteenth century, had rigid tines fitted with coiled spring mountings, guarded by patents. They were easy to adjust and operate but likely to wear out quickly and often in need of repairs — as was the case with most equipment with numerous complex parts. There were two cranked axles to regulate and maintain the working depth, operated by separate levers from the central driving seat. One wheel could be lowered to run in a furrow, while the other ran on the upper land surface, the main axle and the base of the machine always remaining parallel. It could be fitted with an expanding frame and additional levers to serve as a horse hoe, three-drill grubber or ridger. It was mounted on two large wheels and drawn by a single horse between shafts, although when used for ridging a forecarriage steering device was sometimes added.

The semi-grubber was something of a hybrid between grubber and cultivator. On the original grubber the tines were noted for their fixed pitch, changeable only through parallel lift of the entire framework. With the semi-grubber, although tines were set in the earlier manner, outwardly resembling the true grubber, they could be rotated individually, each one having its own axis for improved setting. There were three wheels; two large ones at the rear were mounted on bell cranks and had a row of tines in front of them and a row of tines at the back. The tine bars were operated by levers, raised and lowered from a central driving seat, there being a lever for each bar. There was ample clearance between the tines, and the semi-grubber was considered a good machine for rough ground and foul conditions.

Rollers or rolls

These primitive forms of clod crushers and ground levellers were among the earliest farm implements ever used. They could be made from stone, wood, iron or concrete; later types were sometimes hollow and filled with water for extra weight. Some of the earliest types were made from the trunks or larger branches of felled trees, stripped only of their twigs and smaller branches while the bark was left intact. There are also early examples of wooden rolls bound with iron rings and shod with deep spikes. Rolls are also worked in sections of several attached together, covering a wider area than a single roll. These needed large teams of horses or oxen to pull them. The single roll had either a single horse in shafts or two horses in tandem, the lead horse in chains or connected to the shaft horse by traces.

The Cambridge roll, named after its makers, was a ring roller made up of numerous equally spaced rings or ridges. It was used in the preparation of seedbeds and never for rolling and levelling grassland. Rollers could be riding or walking implements but were usually the latter. The riding roller was mainly used for parks or sports grounds rather than farmwork.

One of the main functions of a roll was to make the ground level, smooth and even, both before and after ploughing and harrowing.

Fig. 17. Types of roller or leveller.

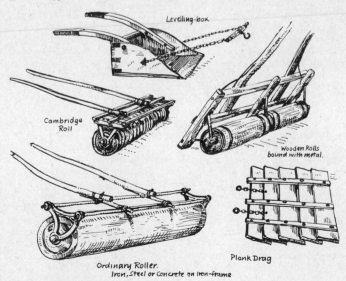

Levelling-box

Cambridge Roll

Wooden Rolls bound with metal.

Ordinary Roller. Iron, Steel or Concrete on Iron-frame

Plank Drag

Harrows

Harrowing was another simple means of breaking up the clods of soil to form a seedbed and also of covering the seed once it had been broadcast. Like the plough and the roller it is of great antiquity. Horse-drawn harrows appear in many illuminated manuscripts and the Bayeux Tapestry of 1080. For the shallow ploughing of certain grain crops it was sufficient to broadcast the seed and then to drag a spiked harrow over the sown areas. Harrows were usually less cumbersome and heavy than cultivators or grubbers and used on lighter soils.

The original or Roman harrow was little more than a sledge with iron spikes on the underside. This was replaced by the Saxon and Norman harrow or beam harrow, made from large balks of roughly hewn timber –– usually oak — also with iron spikes. Versions of this type were used until the eighteenth century and after. At first all the spikes or prongs were straight, but later some were curved and splayed at the tips, and these are called duck-footed. Eventually there were harrows with round, straight, chisel and duck-footed points; round points had greater penetration for lighter draught while the duck-foot, in particular, needed greater

Fig. 18. Beam-type drag harrow.

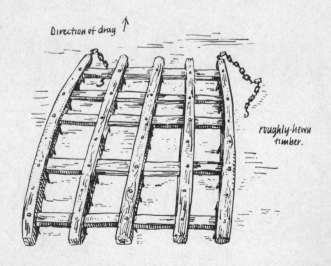

Direction of drag ↑

roughly-hewn timber.

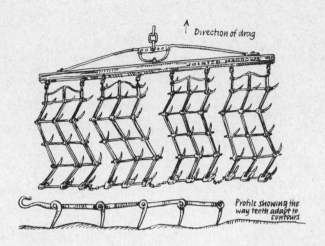

↑ Direction of drag

JOINTED HARROW

Profile SHOWING the way teeth adapt to contours

Fig. 19. Jointed or zigzag harrow.

draught power and was of heavier than average construction. A wooden harrow fitted entirely with hoe blades was introduced during the early nineteenth century by Lionel Haywood of Suffolk, and this was known as the extirpator.

While some harrows depended on fixed wooden members or metal crossbeams, often with a mixed selection of spikes, later types (especially those mass-produced during the nineteenth century) were in zigzag sections bolted, linked or chained together, known as chain harrows. The chain harrow was often of heavy circular links covering and crushing by weight alone. Teeth or spikes on harrows varied between 5 and 10 inches (125 and 250 millimetres) in length and were several inches apart. A heavy or coarse pattern was needed on rough ground and clay soil. With some modern harrows, which have a weight of 10 pounds (4.5 kilograms) per tooth, the spikes or curved prongs—according to type—could be raised by levers on the harrow. A typical harrow of the late 1890s had lever- and spring-operated spring teeth (curved prongs) and was a fairly large riding implement. It had two parallel frames each with bars (three in number), supporting six to eight teeth, spikes or prongs on each side, which were raised or

21

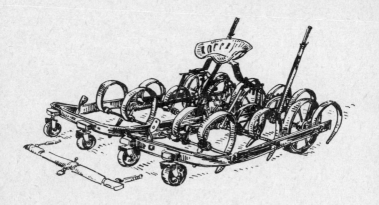

Fig. 20. Spring-tooth riding harrow.

lowered by hand levers. It was supported by eight small land wheels, there being four spoked wheels at the back and four disc wheels at the front. This type was known as an adjustable harrow.

The disc harrow, less frequently used in Britain than in North America and colonial countries, was an American invention of the mid nineteenth century. It had a set of heavy metal discs, curved or convex, in two sets of six per side. They were set at adjustable angles, inclined as though sloping upwards and outwards. This was a riding implement with a high spring seat, drawn by a team of several horses, the number of the team depending on the heaviness of the soil.

What appears to have been a compromise between harrow and roller was the plank drag, sometimes known as a rubber. It consisted of at least five planks of thick, heavy timber, overlapping at the edges like the clinker build of certain sailing ships and boats. It was dragged over ploughland by a single horse and could be weighted as required although the planks were usually considered heavy enough on their own account. At one period there was also a heavy barrow-like box, made of rough timbers, to contain weights such as heavy stones. It was drawn by a single horse and served much the same purpose as the plank drag. It had curved steering handles at the rear, not unlike the stilts of a plough. This was usually known as a levelling box.

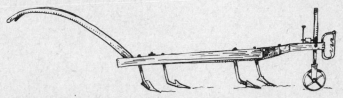

Fig. 21. Early single-horse hoe with wooden beam.

3. Hoes

Hoeing weeds between the rows of growing crops was an essential part of husbandry, especially before the advent of chemical sprays and weedkillers. This could be done by hand or by horse-drawn machinery and the latter was made much easier to use by the evenly spaced rows of machine drilling, as opposed to haphazard methods of broadcasting. Early horse hoes, drawn by a single horse in chain traces attached to a spreader or whippletree, were usually made of stout wooden beams on a wedge-shaped or triangular plan. The whippletree was connected to a hook or hake at the fore end, while there were two handles at the rear similar to the stilts of a plough. Forward terminations of the hooks or tines were splayed out in characteristic hoe shapes, these penetrating the full depth of each beam supporting them. A similar hoe was eventually made of iron throughout, a factory product rather than the work of a local blacksmith and carpenter working in cooperation. Both types of implement had a small adjustable

Fig. 22. Iron-framed one-row hoe.

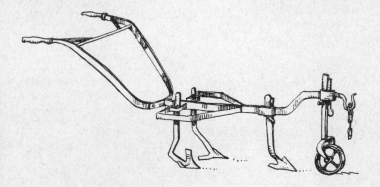

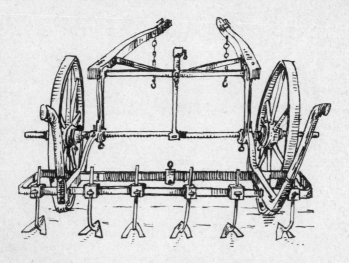

Fig. 23. Martin's general-purpose hoe, rear view.

wheel supporting the fore end of the frame. Larger hoes were later introduced which could be converted, through minor adjustments, into cultivators, often mounted with a riding seat and land wheels.

The purpose of the hoe was to tear out and expose the roots of weeds, which died after exposure. It thus prevented the crop from being smothered and greatly increased both quantity and quality of yield. It was an important process of cultivation in the European vineyards and formed the basis for both the method and treatise of Jethro Tull, mentioned further in the next chapter. Without efficient hoeing the work of ploughing, harrowing, sowing and rolling would have been wasted effort.

4. Drilling machines

Machines for sowing and the regular distribution of seed, grain and manure are popularly associated with the great agricultural developments of the eighteenth century. Yet crude drills and dibbles were known to several early civilisations, especially in India, China and Japan, several thousand years before they were accepted in Europe. There were two main forms of Chinese seed drill, one of which resembled a small plough and the other a form of barrow. Both had hollow teeth or tubes which led from containers above the wheels, dropping seeds in rows between 7 and 14 inches (180 - 350 millimetres) apart. Gabriel Platte, writing during the mid seventeenth century, described a dibbling machine (used for making holes into which seeds were placed) on which iron pins were made to play up and down in the soil 'like virginal jacks'. Some years later a man named Worlidge wrote concerning a seed drill on four equal or equirotal wheels, of which he appeared to have been the inventor, but this was little used or noticed. The diarist John Evelyn commented, about the same period, on the use of a Sembrador or continental drilling machine in several European countries. This may have influenced Jethro Tull, a country gentleman living in semi-retirement, by whom the first workable English seed drill was introduced about the year 1701. The machine by Worlidge was not a practical success.

Yet if Tull was not the sole originator of the seed drill, his version, made by local blacksmiths, may be considered the most efficient type used in Britain up to the late Stuart period. Although born and reared in the country, Jethro Tull graduated at Oxford and was later called to the bar, his main diversion being the study of church music and playing the organ. The life of a London barrister, however, did not suit his health and he returned to the country for the sake of better air and relaxation. He could not remain idle for long and found an interest, among other things, in working a small farm, playing the organ in the parish

Fig. 24. Cross-section of early seed drill.

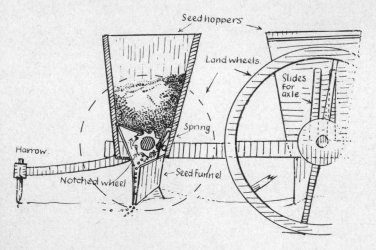

25

Fig. 25. Jethro Tull's drill.

church on Sundays. It was while staring at the organ pipes, perhaps during an over-long sermon, that he was first inspired to experiment with a seed drill. It occurred to him that something very like the narrow pipes, with their pointed ends, might well be mounted on wheels to make the sowing of seeds both deep and regular. Tull's drill was used as part of a system of cultivation outlined in his later book — a classic of agricultural science — on 'Horse Hoeing', published some years later. Tull considered drilling — for which he is mainly remembered — as secondary to the importance of sound hoeing techniques. The Tull drill of 1701 or 1702 was not at first widely accepted, as there was no shortage of cheap labour in a semi-feudal society.

The advantage of drilling over the earlier methods of broadcast sowing was the combined speed, depth and regularity with which the work could be accomplished. Tull's drill had four land wheels, with two large wheels at the front, the axles of which could be adjusted or raised on vertical slides, and two smaller wheels at the back. There were three boxes that fed seed into the tubes, sheats or droppers, each of which had a forward thrusting coulter or foot making a channel into which the seed would fall. A harrow attachment at the rear of the machine was dragged behind to cover the open drills. Before entering the tube, seeds fell on to a grooved cylinder, checked by a spring-held tongue, allowing them to be planted evenly and separately in depressions made by the coulter. The machine could sow 3 tons of seed at one session and was able to make drills and both fill and cover them in the same operation, with great saving in manpower. This led to a local strike of farm-workers, which tended to make other farmers and landowners wary of using such methods, while tenant farmers knew that too many improvements would only lead to increased rents. It was the changing economic and social conditions towards the end of the eighteenth century that proved the greatest incentive towards limited but universal farm mechanisation.

Throughout the eighteenth and nineteenth centuries there were almost as many different designs for seed drills as there had been for ploughs. Two outstanding examples were the double drill plough of Sir John Anstruther of Edinburgh and the four-wheeled drill or plow (plough) invented by the Reverend William Ellis of Hertfordshire. Both of these were fairly light and guided from the rear. The Ellis drill (1745) had a manure hopper for fertilisers.

Cooke's drill

This was invented by the Reverend James Cooke of Heaton Norris near Manchester in 1788 and later improved by a Norfolk farmer named Henry Baldwin. It may be described as the prototype of all good modern drills used up to the tractor age. One of its main features was an unusual seedbox, the rear of which was much lower than the forepart. The interior was fitted with partitions, supported by adjustable bearings to make the delivery of seeds equal and regular, especially when passing over uneven ground. The feeding cylinder revolved by means of toothed wheels, the outer surface of the cylinder being provided with small cups that revolved with the wheel, of different sizes according to the size and type of seed to be planted. With each turn of the cylinder seeds were deposited in the tubes, which were in three rows behind three forward-pointing but separate coulters. By using an expanding or sliding axletree more land could be covered, allowing the use of an extra seedbox and coulter. Self-regulating levers were attached to coulters, hanging each coulter on a separate lever at right angles to the crossbars of the framework. The levers—swinging on hinged joints—had a moveable weight at the opposite end that pressed the coulter into the soil at variable levels—by independent action—according to the lie of the land.

Fig. 26. Cooke's first drill.

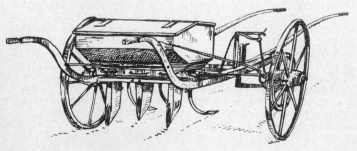

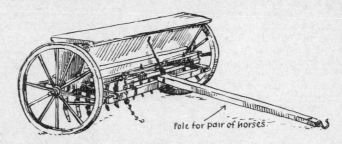

Fig. 27. Suffolk drill, front view.

The Suffolk drill

This was a further improvement on Cooke's drill, with additions and modifications made by the brothers Smythe, who farmed at Swefling and Peasenhall. It could be adapted for sowing a wide range of different seed types and also for drilling manure — with the addition of a fertiliser box or manure hopper. A special device was also used for adjusting the distance between the coulters, with extra facilities for drilling very small seed. It was a four-wheeled machine with a swing-steerage mechanism on the forecarriage, operated by a man in attendance walking at the side of the drill, who could move the coulters to left or right as desired. There were also general improvements in the gearing of the land wheels and the barrels from which the seeds fell into the coulter tubes.

The Kent drill

A four-wheeled drilling machine also known as the Four Share Corn, Bean and Seed Drill, the Kent drill was introduced about 1810 and still used, with modifications, until the 1940s. Similar in many aspects to the Suffolk drill it had an adjustable forecarriage to suit the width of planting rows. The seedbox was placed above the smaller wheels of the forecarriage, having a cup-feed mechanism in which seed fell from the hopper-like containers on to rotating discs fitted with small cups, lifting seeds—in the course of their revolution — into the narrower containers or undertins (tins). The first or upper part of these was known as the rear-upper cranked conductor tube, from which seed passed into the lower coulter tubes. The tubes were cranked or articulated for greater flexibility.

Each land wheel of the machine had a narrow iron tyre which fitted into depressions or ferrules on the sturdy wooden spokes that closely resembled those of an old-fashioned wheelbarrow, seeming out of proportion with the rims. The junction of the narrow rims — of either round or square section — was not only to carry and roll the machine but to mark out a track for the driver (walking at the rear) to follow. The driver or steersman controlled the machine by means of large wooden handles set at the rear. There was also a lever mechanism for raising the coulters on reaching the end of each row and for road travel.

Garrett's drill

An improved general-purpose drill introduced by the firm of Garretts of Leiston in Suffolk during the mid nineteenth century, this drill could be used — with various adjustments — for drilling corn seed, grass seed, mangolds and turnips. Manure could be delivered with the seed, through either the same or separate pipes, by means of a double-action stirring mechanism, with both revolving and perpendicular motion, that prevented manure from clogging the outlets. The amount of manure dropped by the machine could be regulated manually by working a slide under the lower aperture of the manure box. For straightforward corn or grass drilling the manure box could be removed, as an unnecessary burden.

Fig. 28. Garrett's drill, rear view.

The delivery of seeds by other types of drilling machine tended to be less regular when moving down a slope or changing to an uphill direction. A sudden change in position or speed of the drill often caused tremors, tipping more seed down the tubes than was needed. This was greatly remedied in Garrett's machine by having two cogwheels at opposite ends of the seed barrels or containers, for working at different speeds. Either of these could be put in or out of gear as required to adjust speed of delivery.

The Bedfordshire drill

This was invented by Robert Salmon working for the Duke of Bedford on the home farm at Woburn Abbey during the early nineteenth century. It was later improved by two brothers named Batchelor, farming at Lidlington near Bedford. Other modifications were made by Hensman of Woburn and Smith of Kempston, all in the county of Bedfordshire. In this type the seedbox rested above two centres on either side of its framework, between which it swung to keep a level position in moving over the land area. This movement could be controlled by a steersman walking alongside via a screw and crank mechanism. Seed corn was deposited into the delivery tubes by iron cups on circular plates centred on spindles or axles connected to the nave of one or other of the land wheels. Coulters were pressed into the ground by the weight of the undercarriage and framework of the machine. Steerage was by means of two rearward projecting wooden bars, attached to the axletree of the land wheels. These were further connected by a crossbar with four small handgrips (two each side), for greater accuracy of control. There were from four to eight coulters on this type of drill, those with the largest number being used on light and level land only.

Fig. 29. Bedfordshire drill.

Force-feed drills

A later type of drill used the force-feed technique, the seed falling through apertures of the seedbox or hopper into funnels, through each of which a shaft projected, supported on a bowl-shaped wheel. The wheels were either cogged or grooved inside to feed seed into the tubes with great regularity and precision. Instead of a coulter at the lower end of each tube there was a revolving disc similar to the discs of certain harrows.

Maize or corn listing machines

Maize, known in the United States as Indian corn, was planted by a two-wheeled riding machine known as a corn planter or listing machine or engine. 'List' means a single row for planting purposes. It resembled a sulky plough, having a high seat and two land wheels, and was drawn by a pair of horses, one on either side of a draught pole. Under the framework was a disc coulter and ploughshare fitment — the latter having a double mouldboard turning a furrow equally right and left. To the rear of the mouldboard was a deep prong or foot known as a subsoiler and directly behind this was a tube leading from the seedbox, behind the riding seat. The feed plate or mechanism was operated by shafted gears of the nearside wheel (land wheel). Soil was neatly worked back into the furrows covering the newly planted seed by two fixed shovels or scoops connected to the rear of the machine by extension bars.

Bean drills

Beans were frequently planted by dual- or multi-purpose drills or by the use of smaller, less impressive types than those previously mentioned. The average bean drill had a barrow-like framework, frequently used manually as a wheelbarrow rather than a horse-drawn implement, although like every other type of machine it could be adapted for horse or pony draught. The seedbox and (often) single coulter tube inclined forward, mounted behind two large wooden handles or stilts.

Turnip drills

Turnip-sowing drills or machines often consisted of a hefty pair of single shafts supporting a pair of seedboxes or hoppers at the rear end for double row planting. The drill pipes were preceded by two conical or hollowed-out rolls, one on each side, to smooth and contain the ridges necessary for this type of planting. These were

Fig. 30. Turnip sowing machine or drill.

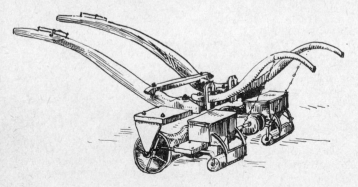

followed in many cases by smaller and flatter rolls further back to help cover the seeds.

The drop drill

This was a two-wheeled, usually two-horse machine perfected by Garretts of Leiston, in which seed was delivered down a flexible many-jointed tube. The lowest tube section had an oscillating movement above a small platform, rather like the swing of a pendulum. When the machine was at rest the platform or lid closed tightly against the aperture, which opened automatically as the drill moved forward. Material accumulating inside the tube was flung out in oscillations, breaking the normal continuity of planting and sowing in detached irregular patches, where this was needed. It usually fed out a mixture of seed and fertiliser.

The mechanical dibble or dibbler

The original dibble, still used in garden and allotment, was a pointed stick for planting seeds. In farming, before the widespread use of drills, this was done by teams of men and women. To dibble wheat the furrows were broken up and rolled down fairly flat and the dibblers walked backwards along the rows in a crouching position, making dibble holes, both to right and left, with both hands clutching dibble sticks. Each dibbler was followed by a dropper, who filled each hole with two or more seeds. A single dibbler could normally cover half an acre (0.2 hectares) per day in good weather. Dibblers and droppers were followed by men with rolls or harrows.

The mechanical dibbler was either a manual or horse-drawn machine. As the dibbles were pushed into the ground with an up and down motion, cups collected seeds from a hopper and fed these down hollow tubes into the previously made dibble hole.

Mechanical or controlled broadcasters

Despite the ever increasing variety of drilling machines, broadcasting of seed continued on some farms until the early twentieth century. Originally a farmworker would walk up and down the furrows casting handfuls of seed alternately right and left by skilful guesswork. A later improvement of this method was the use of the seed fiddle, invented in the United States and introduced to Britain, through Liverpool, during the early nineteenth century. This depended on the horizontal movement of an arm or bow across the front of the person carrying the machine, which was merely a box and sack held under the arm, from which seed fell by gravity into the bow section. Working the machine resembled the act of fiddling or playing the violin. Cheap and easy to work, this made broadcast sowing more reliable than hitherto but was no match for the seed drill. Later during the nineteenth

1. *Ploughing and drilling with horses in Hampshire.*
2. *Ploughing with horses.*

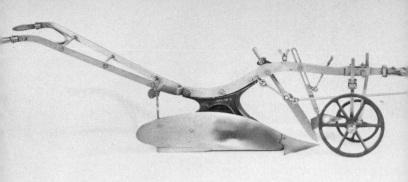

3. A wheel plough with a skim coulter, or miniature ploughshare, mainly used where there is stubble or old vegetation to bury, often before deep ploughing.

4. A wooden-framed plough drawn by a pair of oxen in Essex about 1890. The ploughshare is supported on road wheels.

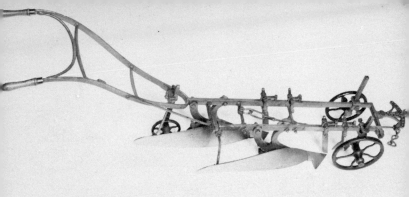

5. A double-furrow plough. Early multi-furrow ploughs required so many oxen or horses to pull them that turning at the headlands was a very awkward manoeuvre.

6. Three horses at work with a multi-furrow plough in Hampshire. The chain traces and whippletrees of the draught gear can be clearly seen.

7. Martin's cultivator of the late nineteenth century had easily adjustable rigid tines fitted with coiled spring mountings.

8. A Cambridge roll at work in the Cotswolds. Made up of numerous equally spaced ridges, it was used in the preparation of seedbeds.

9. Harrowing with a rigid-framed harrow.

10. Worlidge's drill, in the late seventeenth century, was one of the earliest machines for sowing seed but was not adjudged a success in practice.

11. Jethro Tull's seed drill, invented in 1701-2, was inspired by the pipes of a church organ.
12. The drill invented by the Reverend James Cooke in 1788 was the prototype of all good drills used until the tractor age.

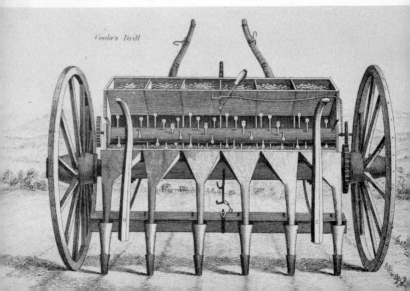

Cooke's Drill

13. Drilling with a pair of horses.

14. Drilling on heavy land with a four-horse team.

15. A single-wheel machine for broadcasting seed.
16. The reaping machine invented by the Reverend Patrick Bell and first produced in 1826 was propelled from behind by the horses. It was little used in Britain.

century there was a semi-mechanised version of the broadcast method in which an oblong cylinder or seed hopper with apertures on the underside was mounted in a transverse or crosswise position on a two-wheeled carriage behind a single horse. It could swivel sideways to pass through gates or down narrow lanes at the end of a day's work. Some machines of this type, also drawn by a single horse, had double or latitudinal cylinders mounted in parallel, one on either side of the machine, although these were less popular than the less expensive transverse (single-box) design. The apertures were opened and closed by gearing from the land wheels.

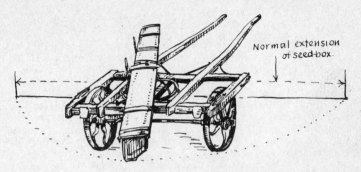

Fig. 31. Broadcast hoe, on swivel for passing through gates.

5. Harvesting machinery

Early reaping machines

Although hand mowing and harvesting were universal from prehistoric times to the mid nineteenth century, the first reaping machine was invented by the Romans, described by Pliny in AD 31 and even earlier by Palladius. This was a two-wheeled cart or carriage pushed by a yoke of oxen from the rear, although sometimes by a single ox. A number of keen blades were fitted to the front of the machine, fixed to a frame and regulated by a man walking alongside. The blades cut the ears or grain-bearing parts of the corn, which fell back on to the rear platform. The oxen were driven into the standing crop and such appliances were only used when there was a glut of natural straw. It was considered, like steam ploughing of a later age, to be a great advantage only with open fields of flat regular shape.

The manual reaping hook, usually a toothed or true sickle, and later the scythe held sway for centuries, although during the 1780s

Fig. 32. Early type of reaper driven into the corn.

and 1790s there were several attempts at mechanisation. The first of these was a reintroduction of the Roman machine, with modifications, by a Mr Capel-Lloft of Bury St Edmunds. This was followed by the experiments of a farmer named Smith of Deanston, who was responsible for several working models and a full-scale reaping machine, the latter not appearing until 1811. Another version of the same machine, although improved, appeared in 1813. Both were based on the operation of a rotary knife that cut the corn fairly low on the stalk, first drawing it aside with a gathering rake that revolved in unison with the blade. In the second version corn was fed against a large central drum, slightly above the level of the knife, that swept it round and aside to fall in even lines at the side of the machine. Smith's reaping machines, although a great step forward, were considered ungainly, awkward in cornering and likely to fail on uneven land.

Other early inventors in this field were Boyce and Plucknet, the former introducing a device of horizontally revolving scythe blades, while the latter constructed a machine like a circular saw, also on the horizontal plane. With most early machines there was little or no attempt at laying or gathering the crop, and the cut corn fell in untidy heaps. It was Robert Salmon of Woburn, pioneer of the Bedfordshire drill, who invented the shears method of harvesting, later used for both corn reaping and grass cutting.

During the early 1820s there were various experiments made by Henry Ogle of Northumberland and John Mann of Cumberland, working in friendly rivalry on opposite sides of the Pennines. Ogle was a schoolmaster at Rennington, working in conjunction with a small iron master, who owned a forge at Alnwick. Ogle supplied the ideas while Brown, the iron master, was the more practical partner, responsible for casting the parts and erecting the prototype. This was different from most of its predecessors as it was drawn by horses rather than pushed from behind by horses or oxen and could be guided with greater speed and accuracy than other types. It had a sharp vibrating blade attached to the offside of the undercarriage and this moved from left to right by means of a guiding crank. Very little was heard of the machine after its demonstration and it may be concluded that it proved too expensive to manufacture and maintain in prevailing conditions. Mann's reaper had a polygonal knife for cutting and a series of attached rakes for making a neat swath. Mann took nearly ten years to perfect the prototype, which was brought to public notice at an agricultural show held during the late summer of 1832. Although successful in cutting a nearby oatfield in record time it received neither the expected premium nor the least encouragement from the panel of judges, after which the inventor lost interest and turned to other projects.

Patrick Bell's reaping machine

Most of the early machines, although ingenious, had several drawbacks in either construction, operation or expense. The first truly practical reaping machine was constructed by the Reverend Patrick Bell, a Scottish nonconformist minister living at Carmyllie, Angus (Tayside). This incorporated several devices still used on the modern binder, stripper and combine harvester. In order to keep the development of his machine a close secret, Bell worked behind locked doors and even the first trials were held in a barn, where a quantity of standing corn had been grown for the purpose. Other experiments were carried out in a wheatfield some distance from the nearest roads, at dead of night. The corn was cut by rows of double-edged blades driven by rods or bars geared

Fig. 33. Patrick Bell's reaper.

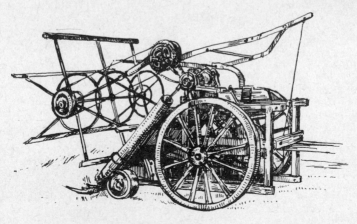

to land wheels of the machine. Like the machines of Lloft, Boyce and Plucknet it was propelled from behind by two horses, these working abreast on either side of a draught pole. It lumbered head on into the crop, stalks of which were forced into the blades by revolving slats, then falling on to an apron or tray inclined diagonally in front of the machine. Rows or swaths of neatly cut corn were laid alongside the track of the reaper, to be collected and made into sheaves by harvest women following behind. This was not a riding machine, its driver walking at the rear nearside to control the horses. Being fairly heavy for its size it ran on four wheels, the leading pair being little more than solid discs or rollers while the larger rear wheels resembled those of a cart or light wagon, having cast iron naves and twelve spokes each. On a good day it was possible to cut 14 acres (5.7 hectares) using a work force of two draught horses, a driver to look after them, and from twelve to fourteen men or women to bind, collect and stack the sheaves for drying. Although awarded a small premium at the Royal Highland Society Show and highly commended by the Royal Agricultural Society, there was no immediate rush to order the machine and very little capital for its development or marketing. It first appeared in 1826 and several were used for corn harvests of

Fig. 34. Self-raking reaper.

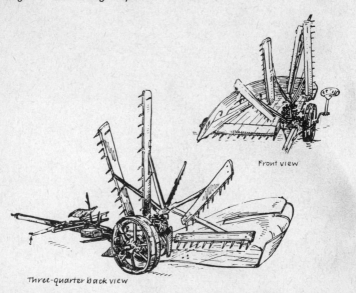

Front view

Three-quarter back view

the early 1830s, made for Bell at a small factory in Dundee, although he is thought to have made very little money from the project. At least four of the Dundee machines found their way to the United States, where, like many other European inventions, they were better appreciated than in the land of their origin.

The sail reaper

Developments in England at a slightly later period included the three-horse (push-type) reaping machine with a side-delivery mechanism. This was eventually harnessed to a steam-driven engine constructed by Aveling and Porter, although the prototype may be credited to Crosskills of Beverley in Humberside. In some later designs, a few still used well into the twentieth century, the horizontally revolving slats at the front or side of the machine were replaced by diagonally inclined sails, the edges of which were armed with the tines or teeth of a rake, on one side only. This version was known as the self-raking sail reaper, although, to confuse matters further, the slats on the Bell machine, and later on the reapers of McCormick, were also known as sails. It was invented by J. and E. Howard of Bedford during the 1860s and when superseded for wheat harvesting it was still used for flax, clover and buckwheat, as these crops were often shattered by the action of a binder. The machine consisted of an almost semicircular wooden tray angled above the cutting blades, from which corn was swept by the sails, which were operated by bevel gearing on the offside of a massive land wheel. The driving seat was to the left of the wheel or on the nearside.

Cyrus McCormick and developments in America

In America a more compact and better planned reaping machine was introduced by Cyrus McCormick of West Virginia (then part of the original state of Virginia), who constructed a prototype in 1831. Some ideas, however, were borrowed from his father, Robert McCormick (also an inventor of agricultural machinery), while both father and son may have been influenced by Bell's machine during the late 1820s. The first McCormick reaper was drawn by a single horse between shafts, attached to the offside of the machine, although later and much heavier versions of the same reaper used two, three and even four horses. The first machine was in the form of a travelling platform on two wheels, at least one of which was fitted with spuds or slats to aid traction by digging well into the ground as they revolved. The wheels also provided motion for the blades through gearing. The knife board was placed at right angles to the rest of the machine, well in advance of the undercarriage. Its blades or fingers were triangular sections, travelling backwards and forwards in the slots or guides of a frame, with a shearing rather than a clipping action.

Fig. 35. Cyrus McCormick's first reaper.

Revolving slats, sails or paddles pressed the stalks against the
cutting blades. The cut grain had to be removed from the platform
by a man walking alongside with a rake. In 1851 a heavier version
was introduced, usually drawn by two horses, driven from a high
seat placed above the geared land wheel on the offside. The single
horse of earlier machines was ridden by a man like a postilion. On
the later machine a man was still needed to rake the grain from
the tray but was provided with a seat, on the nearside, which he
rode astride like a saddle, with his back to the driver and direction
of travel. The first reapers sold for as little as £10 or £12 each but
were not easily sold even at these low figures. An efficient self-
raking device was incorporated into the third production model,
invented by a house-bound invalid named Atkins, whose interest
was stimulated through watching reaping machines at work from
his bedroom windows.

The work of the McCormicks, father and son, came at a for-
tunate time. Their machines did not sell quickly during the early
years but after a decade of trial and error, during which the
machines were greatly improved, there was a sudden labour
shortage due to the California gold rush. Underpaid workers left
farm and workshop to seek a new life or easy fortune in the far
west, and farmers in the eastern states were greatly hampered by
lack of experienced labour. Even so it was nearly twenty years
before the widespread acceptance of reaping machines. Cyrus
McCormick founded one of the largest companies for producing
farm equipment ever known. Backed by the skill and enterprise of
a factory team and enthusiastic sales staff, based on a new plant
opened in Chicago, he was able to exhibit his reaper at the Great
Exhibition of 1851 (held in Hyde Park, London) with the greatest

confidence. His example was followed by another American firm of Hussey and Company, which divided the British, British colonial and European markets with McCormick long before other firms became aware of the potential. The first Hussey reaper was introduced during the 1830s but was greatly improved by a man named Dray, so that it was known by 1851 as Dray's Hussey Reaper. An English Dray Company was established in London for sales and distribution purposes. With the Hussey machine a man sat sideways on a box in the centre, pushing unbound sheaves of corn off a side platform with a rake. By the mid 1860s reaping with horse-drawn machinery was commonplace and hand reaping survived only on remote hill farms and to open a path for the machine.

Mechanical binders

The binder was a further attempt at reducing labour costs in the harvest field and the logical next stage of development. The first workable experiment in this direction was made by an American named Marsh in 1858. His machine caught the cut stalks in revolving canvas webs that carried them to a table further back, where they could be bound into more permanent sheaves. It was still, however, a costly and far from foolproof operation, depending on accurate timing and two active men, apart from the driver. The American firm of Walter A. Wood and Company during the 1870s introduced a wire binder, which although an

Fig. 36. Reaper-binder.

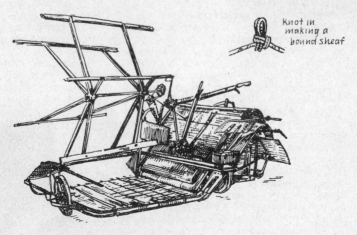

Knot in making a bound sheaf

47

advance on the early machines was still slow and costly. Binding with string or special binder twine was invented by an Englishman named F. J. Appleby, who used a mechanism that was popular on most farms for over a hundred years. This knotted each sheaf or bundle of cut corn with strong, simple loops, casting them aside in rows for building into stooks. The reaper binder which not only cut the corn but also made and bound the sheaves was a great timesaver, always an advantage in the variable conditions of the British harvest season. It was a riding machine with a sprung seat on the offside and working parts checked by hand levers in a curved rack of the upper framework. There was a large geared land wheel under the arched framework, with a smaller supporting wheel attached to the platform behind the finger bar. When the machine was dragged to a distant cornfield by road the ¹and wheels were jacked clear of the ground and replaced by road wheels, lowered into place for a sideways-on tow.

The stripper and the combine harvester

The stripper, which took the ears of grain, leaving the stalks, and the combine harvester mainly replaced the reaper binder during the 1890s but were much later in reaching the smaller farms and fields of Britain. They were first used in North America, Australia and the French colonial areas of North Africa but were not accepted in England until the end of the Second World War. The combine is both a reaping and a threshing machine in a single unit, grain emerging at the side husked and ready bagged or suitable for bagging. Although better associated with tractor haulage or self-drive, early types were drawn by up to forty horses or by even larger teams of mules. The animals were controlled from a seat or platform high above the front of the machine and may have represented the largest teams ever driven, apart from those appearing for show in circus parades and carnival processions. Rigs and hitches of this type were first used in the great wheat belt of the American Mid West about 1896. The Canadian firm of Massey-Harris supplied a Tunisian landowner with a grain stripper mounted on a triangular frame between three land wheels and drawn by a team of six oxen or buffalo.

The threshing or thrashing machine, invented by Andrew Meikle during the eighteenth century, was at first a fixed appliance or barn machine. It later became portable and is described in chapter 9. Although some farmers owned threshing machines or boxes, these took up a lot of room and must have been difficult to handle down narrow lanes or in small yards. They were often hired out by contractors, who also provided a fully trained threshing crew. Although many threshing boxes were at first drawn by horse teams most were soon hauled by steam-powered traction engines that also supplied stationary drive in the rick or stackyard.

6. Root lifters

Machines for lifting or harvesting root crops were mounted on two slatted wheels astride the ridges in which the roots were grown and had share-like prongs that dug into the ground, turning the roots out as the machine moved forward. On later types of potato lifter there was a revolving vertical wheel, fixed almost at right angles to the direction of the machine. This had cranks with curved prongs at the extremities that threw out tubers on either side of the demolished ridge. The potatoes were collected by women and children following behind the lifter with buckets. Children were ideal for this work as they are nimbler and nearer the ground than adults. In some areas where there were large potato crops schoolchildren were often given time off to help with the harvesting, especially during wartime, when there was a general shortage of labour. In later years experiments were made with an extension bar and net at the side of the lifter, intended to dispense with the more arduous work. This machine, however, was usually drawn by a tractor rather than by horses.

A machine with revolving blades, arched above the rows, was often used to cut away the green tops or upper parts of a root crop. Blades were inclined diagonally, while land wheels, as with the lifter, were slatted for extra grip. Both topper and lifter were usually drawn by a pair of horses. A type of ridge plough was also used both for making ridges and for digging out root crops. Some of the smaller types used in market and kitchen gardens were hauled manually or by a small pony, although the farm type was drawn by a single horse. Their main characteristic was a double mouldboard or two separate mouldboards for making ridges, throwing up soil both right and left. For digging out roots the body and shares were removed and a single bar with hoe-like blades, fanning out towards the lower extremities, was put in their place.

7. Fertiliser and manure distributors

The type of implement used for spreading fertiliser depended on the kind of fertiliser used, which ranged from powdered and liquid forms to farmyard dung straight from the manure heap or midden. The original method was to take manure on to the land in specially constructed two-wheeled dung carts (often tipcarts), from which it was pitched or tipped in small heaps at convenient intervals, to be spread by men working with forks at ground level. A later invention was the manure distributor, widely known as a muck or dung spreader. This was usually a two-wheeled implement and was drawn by a single horse between shafts. It was widely used from the mid nineteenth century. Manure fell from a transverse box-like hopper on to revolving tines or prongs, which flung it from the rear of the machine, rather like hay from an old-fashioned tedder. There was a less popular, four-wheeled version, drawn by two horses. The use of this machine was known as broadcast manure distributing.

Powdered fertiliser such as bonemeal could be distributed from a large drill mounted between two land wheels in the style of a seed drill, with which it could sometimes double. Manure was often drilled with seed and reference has been made to drill attachments or fittings for this purpose in chapter 4.

Some types of manure drill had large coulters in the form of hollow ploughshares through which the manure was distributed to a considerable depth. The combined manure and seed drill invented by Chandler worked on much the same principle as the bucket dredger, conveying matter fed through a hopper to the coulter tubes via buckets on an endless chain. Chandler's liquid manure cart, of much the same type, could be tipped at various angles by the use of hand-wound mechanism on the shafts.

The use of liquid manures was widespread during the late Victorian era, the commonest forms of distributor being horizontally mounted tanks on two wheels, which could also serve as water carts. These frequently had a rear hand pump as an optional extra. The largest type distributed the manure through pipes connected with a spreadboard and had a tank capacity of up to 220 gallons (1000 litres). Tanks were cylindrical, square or

Fig. 37. Manure distributor.

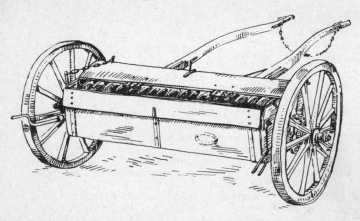

oblong. Chandler's cart took the form of a half cylinder hung between two large wheels on the pivot principle. Some of the larger rectangular types would have a high-perched driving seat, with footboard, at the front of the tank. Most types were pulled by a single horse between shafts, which, apart from the rectangular type, was led rather than driven. Similar water carts were sometimes used by local councils or corporations — in a few cases hired from farmers — for watering roads or bringing water to cottages when the wells had dried up in time of drought. They were also used in bringing water to steam-powered engines working in fields distant from a pump or farm buildings, forming part of the road train for both threshing and ploughing teams.

Fig. 38. Liquid-manure distributor, also used as water cart.

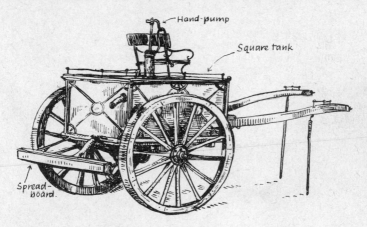

8. Haymaking machinery

After centuries of use of scythe and hand rake mechanisation came suddenly to the hayfield, with horse-drawn implements of every kind from mowing machine to tedder, dump rake and swath turner. The first mowers were used from about 1860, although types of rake and tedder had been used even earlier. All three machines were great savers of time and money and formed part of the equipment on most farms from the 1880s.

The swath turner was introduced in 1896, followed by the side-delivery rake. Both machines, however, were greatly improved by the early 1920s. The elevator, hay loader and hay sweep came shortly before the swath turner. Hay loaders, although invented in 1875, were not widely used until after the First World War.

Horse-drawn and horse-powered machines made it possible to harvest the hay crop almost untouched by hand, except in carting and rick building. They enabled the farmer to take advantage of weather and season, but the haymaking still depended on atmospheric qualities to a considerable extent.

Hay cutting

The best hay was always cut fairly early in the summer, especially during the first days of June. It was then not only more palatable but more digestible and nourishing to livestock than fodder cut even a few weeks later.

The time for cutting was when the hay was in full flower. At a later stage the nutritive content would be much lower, transferred from the leaf and stem to the seeds, which soon become dry and disperse, while the body of the herb turns fibrous, losing the taste of young grass. The younger crop, however, would be lively and lush, harder to stack than old hay but settling tighter in the rick. While yielding more body and weight it also gave place — if the weather was right — to a second growth or aftermath, known in some areas as the eddish.

Mowing machines

The horse mower, always a riding machine with a sprung seat projecting towards the rear, was usually drawn by a pair of horses harnessed on either side of a draught pole. A slightly smaller mower could also be drawn by a single horse or large cob between shafts. The machine was carried on two fairly large travelling wheels, set wide apart and slatted for better grip. Either or both of these were fitted with an inner rim or wheel for nave gearing that drove the cutters or knife blades via a hub gearbox and connecting rod. There were three main parts to the average mower, each of which deserved thorough attention and overhaul. These were the truck or carriage, the cutting blade and bar, and the draught pole with whippletrees or spreaders for attachment to the harness of draught animals. Most cutting bars, especially those used in Britain, were mounted on the right of the driving wheels, for cutting in clockwise rotation. In some countries, however, an anticlockwise cut was preferred.

Small wheels or rollers were used to carry the end of the finger or cutting bar. The angle of the cutting blades could be adjusted and the cutting bar raised or lowered from the driving seat by the use of hand levers, with a foot pedal to put the machine in or out of gear.

The machine was always at its best when new, making a clean cut over the entire length of the finger bar. In this condition the cut was clear and free with little or no trackage left in the stubble. Draught of a new machine in good working order was much

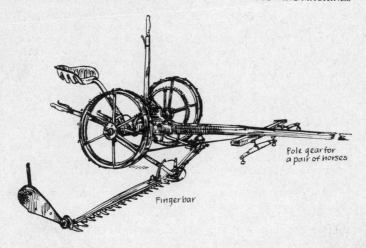

Fig. 39. Grass-cutting or mowing machine.

lighter than with an old mower and the work was quicker, it being said that 'grass fell readily to the knives'.

After a few years even the best machine became heavier and more sluggish, the blades requiring frequent resharpening and adjustment, while the draught might be lowered towards the grass, making haulage more difficult. In consequence the mower might have been scrapped or under repair at the time when it was most needed, often from lack of elementary technical knowledge. Few mowers went for more than three seasons without drastic renovation.

Cutting mechanism

The main working parts were finger bar and blade. Grass was not cut by the blade alone but by the sliding action of the blade on the bar or plate, so that both blade and bar edges needed attention. It was often mistakenly believed that only the blade needed attention to avoid heavy draught, neglect of the machine resulting in an awkward tugging or tearing action.

Blade edges or fingers, in forward pointing wedge or triangular shapes, divided the grass to be cut into neat bunches. Each finger or section of the blade moved from its centre to the centre of the next section and back again, repeating this movement as long as the machine was working in gear. With a reaper or reaper binder the movement was through two finger sections, needing a greater leverage for cutting firmer stalks. In the course of movement each bunch of grass was pressed against the nearest edge of the finger plate, requiring that both edges were not only sharp but in close contact with each other.

The working edge of the finger plate or ledger became dull with constant wear, especially on gritty land or where there was foreign matter in the grass. This caused an imperfect cut with too much grass hanging on the knife and often a sideways pull that reduced draught power. During the working season the ledger or finger plate or bar had to be kept sharpened at the correct angle of bevel. When not in use the machine had to be kept well greased.

Edges of the cutting sections were intended to be in firm contact, like the blades of a pair of scissors. They tended to work loose because of a sagging of the bar, particularly with machines with longer than average bars.

Great stress in the machine was caused by slackness of the knife blades and the consequent general distortion, especially at the inner or connecting end of the bar. This caused the knife to play in its guides, leading to risk of breakage, reduced speed and general inefficiency. One of the most reliable English horse mowers was known as the Albion, made by the firm of Harrison, McGregor and Company of Leigh, Greater Manchester. Its knife-head guide was designed on much the same principle as the crossheads and guides on a steam locomotive and usually gave far less trouble than other mowers. Another reliable early type was Jones's mowing machine, imported to Britain from the United States from the 1890s.

Operation

Before starting to cut it was essential to check the correct height of the pole, necessary for both easy draught and efficient cutting.

Fig. 40. Plan of typical mowing machine.

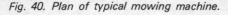

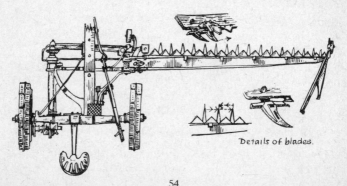

Details of blades.

This was a yard (900 millimetres) from the ground at the head of the pole. The height of the cutting bar was checked by means of a side chain; it had to be taut and at ground level, never lifted very high above the surface of the ground. Driving round corners while the machine was still cutting was a common error, which led to straining and disalignment of the bar. In turning on the square it was necessary either to back the machine or to pivot before starting the next line of cut. As the bar was always well in front of the main axle the horses had to be stopped with the axle opposite and near to standing grass in order to make a pivot. This also prevented strain on the necks and withers (shoulders) of the team.

If the machine was brought to a halt in mid field it was necessary to back away from the crop before restarting, allowing the knife blades to meet their work at good speed in full motion. Power for the cut was transmitted by pawls and gearing, so that a characteristic clicking sound was the sign of a good mower at work. If the sound was irregular and the machine did not start cutting on immediate contact this indicated that pawls were worn down or worked out of shape.

A mower worked hard and fast needed more lubrication than any other farm implement, especially the bearings at the ends of the connecting rod. This part had to be oiled at least every twenty minutes, while bearings at the ends of gear and crank shafts required lubrication every hour. Oil caps had to be kept firmly in place and the whole mechanism washed out with paraffin at least twice a season. Knife blades were sometimes lubricated but they tended to gather grit and dust, leaving a sticky deposit on hay and machine alike.

While a good blade lasted several hours without resharpening, it was always advisable to have spares handy. The resharpening was best done on an old-fashioned grindstone or whetstone, using plenty of water to keep the edges cool. Dry methods, particularly the use of emery wheels, often spoilt the temper of a blade, at least after a number of sharpenings.

On finishing work the pole would either be removed or supported from underneath to avoid strain. The bar was also to be supported by a wooden box or a few bricks covered with sacking. If not to be used for several days, or at the end of a season, the knife was removed and greased. It was desirable to check every working part of a mowing machine at least a month before starting the cutting season.

Draught of mowers

In later years mowers were often made with two speeds, the low speed being for June hay and easy work, while the high speed was for tougher crops later in the season and also for work with slower teams.

The average draught of a two-horse mower was about 3 hundredweights (150 kilograms) with a cut of 4 feet 6 inches (1.37 metres) wide. Working pace was 2½ miles (4 kilometres) per hour. Draught obviously depended on the ratio of gearing but it was generally considered that a good mowing machine cutting early hay needed only a multiplication of twenty, or the flywheel turning twenty revolutions for every revolution of the driving wheels. Old or late hay needed at least thirty revolutions, with a correspondingly increased demand on draught.

Fig. 41. Hay tedder.

Swath turners and tedders

Once the grass had been cut by the mower the real process of haymaking had begun. This was to expose the grass to dry on one side at a time in cut rows or swaths. After a few days it would be turned, originally by men and women with wooden hand rakes but later with a variety of horse-drawn equipment. The swath turner was one of the better known devices, drawn by a single horse and mounted on three iron travelling or land wheels. It was a riding machine with a sprung seat well to the rear, appearing to serve as a form of balance. While the two hindwheels were seven-spoked on geared cranks, the forewheels were much smaller, attached to the mainly tubular framework by stalk and bracket. The hay was turned by curved tines rotating at the ends of cylinders, one on each side of the machine, on which a main shaft led back to gears of the inner wheel hubs. Tines could be raised and lowered by the application of a weighted lever. There was usually a guard on the

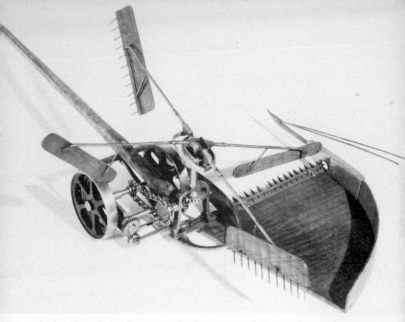

17. *A self-raking sail reaper with four rakes. Invented in the 1860s, it was still used for flax, clover and buckwheat after being superseded for wheat harvesting.*

18. *A reaper binder in action with a three-horse team.*

19. Harvesting wheat with self-binding reapers at Drayton Beauchamp, Buckinghamshire, about 1920.

20. A manure spreader of about 1910 with a sprung box seat for the driver.

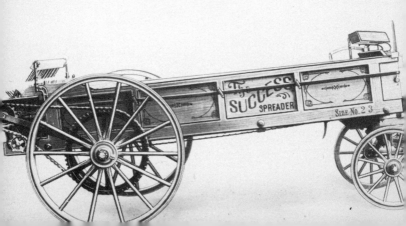

21. A horse-drawn mowing machine at Desford, Leicestershire, about 1930.

22. Haymaking about 1910 near Tring, Hertfordshire, with a horse-drawn mower.

23. The swath turner was a single-horse riding machine used for turning and aerating the mown hay lying to dry where it was cut.

24. Tedding or tidding was a less gentle way of turning hay than swath turning. This is the tedder invented by Robert Salmon.

25. A horse-drawn hay rake of the 1870s. Rakes such as this remained in use even after the tractor replaced the horse.

26. A hayfield scene about 1914. A horse rake is in action while behind are a loaded hay wagon and another wagon waiting to be loaded.

27. *A hay sweep at work in 1925 near Ipswich. It scooped up dry hay from the ground and conveyed it to the stack or wagon.*

28. *A threshing machine of about 1930. It was originally drawn by horses but the shafts have been replaced by a tractor drawbar.*

29. Horse gear for driving a barn threshing machine.

30. Stacking sheaves of wheat in a Dutch barn at Pitstone, Buckinghamshire, about 1920. The elevator is driven by horse gear situated behind the barn.

31. A Marshall portable steam engine. Engines like this powered a variety of machinery on the farm but had to be hauled to the work site by a pair of horses.

nearside attached to a rod leading from the framework. It was possible to turn two swaths at a time, each circle of tines revolving over and above the rows of cut grass, tossing it in the air and allowing the wind to blow through — leaving the swath in a fairly loose mass for greater aeration. Swath turning was considered far gentler than turning the hay by tedding.

The tedder, a version of which is also known as the 'kicker', was either open or closed. In later years the closed or box type was known as a hooded tedder; over the front and part of the top there was a large iron shield, above which there was a driving seat. It derived from an open tedding or 'tidding' machine invented by Robert Salmon of Woburn, comprising two central wheels, between the travelling or land wheels, and having a series of transverse crossbars, mounted with prongs or tines that revolved as the machine moved forward. A later machine had prongs on extension bars pointing in a rearward direction and geared to the land wheels for an elliptical revolution that resembled the backward kick of a horse or mule. Tedders were normally hauled by a single horse between shafts. They were usually riding machines and the seat was partly above the highly dangerous revolving tines, for which reason the protective hood was introduced.

The side-delivery rake of slightly later development was noted for its triple row of tines mounted on cranks and a disc wheel, slightly above ground level. The tines revolved diagonally to the line of travel, the whole structure being mounted on three iron wheels. Two larger wheels at the front end supported the riding seat while an arched framework led back to the single and much smaller rear wheel, the latter on stalk and bracket. It was said to be a development of the horse rake but was more like a cross between the dump rake and the swath turner. It was responsible for gathering rather than turning the hay, converting untidy swaths into neat rows or windrows which were more convenient for

Fig. 42. Side-delivery rake.

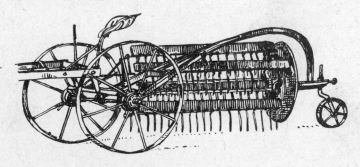

carting or making into small haycocks, for either temporary storage or further drying. Some side-delivery rakes, however, were also used for turning the crop.

Wedlake's hay machine and Ransome's swath rake were similar to tedders, each having adjustable revolving prongs. Wedlake's machine was more complex, having tines in sets of five, spring-mounted in double rows. The swath rake had three sets of much longer and deeper prongs more like those of the conventional dump rake.

Horse rakes

These were widely used from the mid nineteenth century, usually drawn by a single horse, although some were drawn by a pair in double shafts. The latter, however, were more popular in North America and parts of continental Europe. The purpose of the machine was to draw the loosely distributed hay into neat windrows, working backwards and forwards across the entire area of the hayfield.

The most efficient type of rake was invented by James Grant in 1850, descending from the so-called drag rake or heel rake. The large sickle-shaped tines, an invention of James Hart, acted almost automatically. They were raised by slight pressure from a foot pedal or handle lever, easy enough for a boy to work, and fell into place by gravity, the raising motion being assisted by the ratchet and pawl of the travelling wheels. An earlier Scottish rake was based on a wooden framework with much shorter tines operated by a man walking at the rear to raise and depress two wooden handles. Grant's rake and others following the semi-automatic form of operation were essentially riding machines, frequently

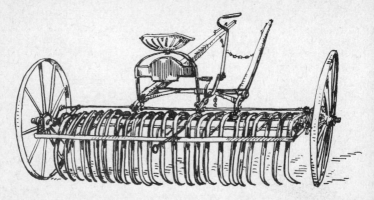

Fig. 43. Horse rake, rear view.

drawn by a fairly light fast-moving horse rather than a lumbering Shire type. The teeth or tines were hinged to a metal frame, points at the lower extremities being about 3 inches (75 millimetres) apart. Being turned inward, they slid under the masses of hay gathering it together ready for dropping or dumping. The width of popular types was 8 feet (2.44 metres) for the inner frame with twenty-four teeth, later increased to 10 feet (3 metres) with thirty teeth and 12 feet (3.66 metres) with thirty-six teeth. The riding seat was balanced in the centre of the arched frame that extended between the travelling or land wheels.

Like several other machines of the hayfield the horse rake outlasted the supremacy of the draught horse and was often towed behind an early tractor, its shafts replaced by a triangular drawbar. Some farmers even used an attachment able to convert shafts into drawbars as a temporary measure so that the same implement might be hauled by either horse or tractor as required.

The later version of the horse rake always had a neat and attractive appearance, painted — like many haymaking and harvesting machines — in bright cheerful colours. While some came to look rusty and neglected out of season, the farmer with a pride in his work made sure they were at least touched up every twelve months, usually repainted at the beginning of the season, a task for wet days in the cart lodge or barn, when there was a lull in other work. Traditional colours were powder blue with dark red wheels or lighter vermilion wheels with a dark green framework.

Hay sweeps and lifts

An American innovation of the 1880s was the hay sweep, although perhaps based on an earlier and smaller reversible rake with teeth or prongs pointing both forwards and backwards, controlled by barrow-like handles, only one set of teeth being engaged at a time. The larger or true hay sweep came to Britain about 1894 and was first used in the flatter and larger fields of the south rather than the north of England. In the north its purpose would also have conflicted with the making of small haycocks. It consisted of a wide framework between two small land wheels, having a forward thrusting row of wooden teeth, each tooth tipped with iron to a depth of 5 inches (125 millimetres). It was drawn by two horses — one on either side of the implement — with the teeth between them. It often had the appearance of being pushed rather than pulled as the teeth were well in advance of the draught animals. The driver was perched on a high central seat behind the framework. It commenced work at the end of a swath or windrow, moving forward at a smart walking pace and collecting hay with a scooping action. When piled with hay it was directed towards the stack and unloaded as though from an ordinary cart or wagon. The amount loaded at each sweep was about two-thirds of a

Fig. 44. Elevator and hay sweep.

normal cart load. Hay could not be swept in this way until it was very dry, as even slightly damp hay tended to form rolls and clog the sweep. Hay sweeps were later propelled by tractors and on some farms pushed by an old car, too battered and run down for road work.

In Scotland and the north of England, subject to more rain than the south, the hay was made into fairly large cocks known by the regional names of ricks, low cocks, pykes and trampcocks, each containing up to 15 hundredweights (760 kilograms) of hay about 10 feet (3 metres) high. They were broad at the base and mainly conical with a high centre point, the whole tending to resemble — from a distance — a straw beehive or skep. These were dotted about the field after the grass had dried in the swath for some time, and were made in the same way as the larger haystack by pitching from the cart. Each cock was left to weather or temper for a number of days or even weeks before the final carting to stack or barn. From the early nineteenth century hay sledges were used (also known as rick lifters) to transport the rick or pyke in one body to the place of final storage. The normal type of sledge used was a low, two-wheeled cart or platform drawn by a single horse between upward curving shafts. This was backed against the side of a rick and the platform tipped at an angle suitable for sliding under its load. A chain was fixed round the base of the rick and this was eventually winched on to the platform using a small rope-operated winch or capstan fixed to the rear end of the shafts on the nearside. The platform of the sledge gradually fell back into position during the winching.

Hay that had to be taken some distance from the fields, perhaps over country roads and through several gateways, was carried in carts fitted with end ladders or extensions to support the overhang. Lifting hay on to the loading platform with pitchforks, especially when the vehicle was high-sided (with protective guards or raves over the wheels) was laborious work. The Americans invented several hay lifters or loaders during the second half of the nineteenth century, although they were not widely used in Britain, except on some larger farms, until the 1920s. They were mounted on large travelling or carrying wheels, being little more than a portable diagonal framework with an endless belt or webs with tines on the upper surface. These picked up the hay at ground level, rotating under protective wooden slats, as the cart to which it was attached moved forward. A man standing in the cart with a pitchfork received the hay from the top of the lift, building the load while on the move.

At the rick or stackyard a larger version of the lifter, known as an elevator, was used for building the final stack, the lower end sometimes having a type of hopper into which hay was fed or placed to keep it in compact masses. Like the lifter it had a continuous web or belt with upward facing tines, but it was much higher than the lifter and mounted on smaller but sturdier land wheels. These were frequently equirotal or much the same size at front and back, while the forewheels of the lifter were much larger than the hindwheels. It could be fitted with shafts or a drawbar at the front end but seldom left the farmyard, where it could be manhandled without too much difficulty, at least for short distances. Drive for the mechanism often came from a horse- or

Fig. 45. Hay sledge.

69

pony-worked gin engine, the animal walking in circles and being attached to a geared drawbar. This appliance was known as horse gears.

Before the introduction of elevators the progressive farmer made use of a horse fork. This was merely a type of grab crane worked over a pulley block, rigged in position with poles and guy ropes. It was operated by a single horse walking backwards and forwards in a straight line. It could lift several hundredweights of hay at a time from a waiting vehicle, cutting out much of the heavy manual work with pitchforks, although not suitable for use with a hay sweep or sledge, needing plenty of body in the load for efficient working of the grab prongs.

9. Portable machines

Portable machines were large items of equipment used in farm and stackyard rather than in the fields or open country. They were stationary while working but frequently were moved from one location to another, often on a seasonal basis, especially when hired out by a contracting firm. In particular, steam ploughing and threshing outfits comprised lumbering road trains, almost like part of a travelling funfair. Other vehicles apart from the working machinery might include a living van, water cart and one or more carts for spare parts and other equipment. The train for steam ploughing also used their ploughing engines as locomotives (traction engines) but even these would have a horse-drawn water cart bringing up the rear of the procession. On the road it might be towed behind another vehicle, using a draught connector instead of shafts, but in places where the steam engines worked some distance from the nearest water supply it had to be horse-drawn, borrowing from the stable of the farmer for whom the contract was undertaken.

Threshing machines

Threshing machines were originally static although the early portables were drawn by horses, many being much smaller than their more recent counterparts. The first practical threshing machine was invented by a Scot named Andrew Meikle in 1786, after two or three earlier but abortive attempts had been made, some with water-powered machinery, much earlier in the century. Corn to be threshed was fed into the machine — ears first — down a feeding board and between two fluted cylinders to the beating drum or cylinder, which was armed with four spars or beaters — parallel with its axle — which had the effect of knocking out the grain by their rotative action. Running at a speed of 230 revolutions per minute, the drum forced loose grain and straw on to a concave sieve below which was a further revolving drum with inner rakes or pegs that rubbed the straw on its concavity while allowing husks to fall into an even lower section. The separated straw was subjected to a thorough rubbing and tossing, to be finally discarded, grain falling on to the threshing floor beneath. This, however, still had to be winnowed or separated from the chaff.

A winnowing device in which arms of the machine rubbed grains against a concave iron framework was added to Meikle's peg-drum thresher in 1800. This was the basis of the early portable machine used by farming communities in all parts of Britain until shortly after the Second World War and general acceptance of the self-powered combine harvester. This could thresh, clean and separate wheat from straw and chaff in one operation. Some were barn machines fixed inside buildings of the farmstead and driven by steam or water power; others were worked by gin engines or horse gears, often requiring as many as four horses to one machine. It was heavy work and only the strongest horses could be used at a time when they were also needed for essential carting. Later, portable types were driven by 6 or 7 horsepower (5 kilowatt) steam engines or by the contractor's towing engine. In an early portable type the machine was mounted on a two- or four-wheeled carriage, to be set up independently on the threshing site; the undercarriage was also used as the base or bed for horse gears. This type could be pulled by a single horse between shafts but the heavier and much later types needed a team of two, three and four

Fig. 46. Threshing machine.

horses, depending on local gradients and road conditions. There were several refinements attached to the later machine, including safety devices, but the basic principles were much the same as those used by Meikle over a hundred years earlier.

The outward appearance of the later threshing machine or box was unmistakable, being in the form of a large rectangular box on road wheels, while cranks, driving wheels and belts projected from and festooned the sides. It was mounted on four large wheels, although the front pair were often small enough to turn under the forecarriage in full lock, necessary in negotiating the tight corners and narrow places of most stackyards, where there would be very little room for manoeuvre. Later types had iron wheels but some had wooden spokes with iron naves and tyres similar to the artillery wheel used for military transport wagons of the period. Colours were usually salmon pink or straw yellow, lined out in darker blues, reds and dark green, with visible ironwork jet black and highly varnished. Rounding boards at the top of the machine often had the name of the manufacturer in bold letters, also typical of the period. From the mid 1930s onwards the lettering was often more restrained or painted out. For those with horse draught there would be double shafts rather than a pole and swingletrees or whippletrees. As the types seen on the roads after 1900 were nearly always drawn by tractors or traction engines

Fig. 47. Cross-section of a threshing box. A: corn feed. B: threshing drum. C: straw shakers. D: collecting board. E: dressing riddle. F: end of chute from E. G: grain spout. H: large blower. I: shut-off lid. J: elevator. K: smutter. L: creeper. M: riddle. N: second blower. O: grain passage. P: upper grain passage. Q: rotary screen. R: classified grain. S: wheel chocks. T: forecarriage. U: rotary screen bush. V: dust spout. W: grain in sacks. X: road wheels. Y: chaff delivery. Z: carvings (broken straw) delivery.

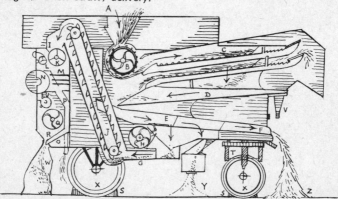

those surviving in odd corners of farmyards or preserved in museums usually have a drawbar at the front end. Some later types also have pneumatic tyres.

Horse-drawn steam engines

From the mid nineteenth century limited use was made, on the larger farms, of portable steam engines, which to the untrained eye resembled the traction engine. The portable engine may be identified at a glance by the absence of a driving platform or footplate, along with the attached fuel bunker, at the firebox end. Portable engines were used on different parts of a large farm or country estate for a variety of purposes from driving threshing machines and circular saws to working all types of barn machinery such as chaff cutters and grinding mills. Like the threshing box they were drawn over country roads by a pair or team of horses (usually the former), attached to the front or smokebox end, in double shafts. On the road the tall funnel would be hinged back or detached for passing under low bridges or the overhanging branches of trees and carried horizontally along the top of the boiler like the funnel of a Thames tug. Some portable engines were used to provide heating systems for the glasshouses of market gardens.

Other horse-drawn equipment

Other equipment drawn by horses from one site to another included the vans and huts for shepherds, used by them at lambing time when they had to eat and sleep away from the farm, often near a remote group of sheep pens on downs or wolds. When shearing equipment replaced hand clipping, the shearing machines — often hand-operated by turning a cranked handle — were sometimes mounted on a spring cart or converted four-wheeled wagonette drawn by a single horse. The shepherd's living van was more like a shack on wheels than the Romany vardo or even the contractor's caravan used by ploughing and threshing teams. They were often made on the farm or by a local craftsman, fitted together from planks of wood and lengths of corrugated iron, using wheels from discarded implements and any old bits and pieces available. A shepherd's hut at Dodington Carriage Museum, Avon, even utilised the bodywork of an old London horse bus, mounted on nondescript iron wheels.

When the stackyard elevator had to be moved any distance this was also work for one or two horses, although it could be manhandled within the farmyard.

10. Horses and harness

There were four main types of heavy draught horse widely used until the mid 1950s, although gradually superseded by tractors and lorries from the late 1920s. Tractors were introduced much earlier on some of the larger farms but it was not until after the First World War that they began to be accepted by the average mixed farmer or smallholder. Among the many reasons for this were the great loss of horses during the First World War, epidemics that destroyed many others some time after the fighting ceased and the great enthusiasm of the rising generation for anything mechanical. During the later stages of the war the British Prime Minister, Lloyd George, asked the Americans to send large consignments of Fordson tractors, and this opened a floodgate in farm mechanisation. There is still work which horses can do better than tractors, on hill farms, associated with forestry and working between rows in orchards and market gardens. For carting and delivery work on short hauls they are much more economical than the internal combustion engine and in some parts of the country there are signs of a revived interest in the horse as an agricultural animal.

The Shire

The most popular of the heavy breeds in England and Wales is the Shire. Although Wales is not usually considered an arable farming area where large numbers of carthorses would be needed, some fine specimens were bred in the limestone country of northern Powys. A large flattish or undulating area between Clun Forest and the Berwyn range was ideal farming country producing a predominantly grey horse that was the equal of the best Shires. Grey horses were not usually popular with pundits of the breed society and in most cases the English Shire of the midlands is bay, black or brown. The ancestor of the Shire is supposed to be the warhorse of the late middle ages and early Tudor period, able to carry an armoured warrior and charge at 'a good round trot', the normal pace in battle of the heavy cavalry. It has been claimed that horses of this type were too precious for use on the land until they were rejected as chargers, with the increased use of gunpowder in battle and a change of tactics. From the sixteenth century onwards cavalrymen needed much lighter and swifter horses and so more of the heavy horses could be spared for farmwork and timber hauling, being quicker and more active for this type of work than oxen. During the eighteenth century the breed was greatly improved by Robert Bakewell of Dishley and much of the finest stock was bred from a remarkable sire of this period known as the Packington Blind Horse, named after the village near Ashby-de-la-Zouch in Leicestershire where he was at stud.

Although not perhaps the largest or the most powerful horses as individuals, Shires are the largest on average and hold many records for pulling weights against the dynamometer. They tended to be slow and ponderous but were usually docile and even-tempered, always an advantage in a working horse. Average height was up to 17 hands (1.73 metres) high. The more rangy modern type is frequently up to 18 hands (1.83 metres) and has a slightly arched neck, Roman nose and thick feather on the lower limbs. The hairy legs of Shires were considered one of their most attractive features and earned high marks in the show ring but induced a condition of greasy leg or grease, almost unknown to other breeds. This was because the long hair soaked up quantities of damp and dirt, especially in winter. The evidence of photographs and descriptions reveals that the Shire has undergone many changes, even during the past thirty years. These reflect aims and ideals of the pundits, often through whims of fashion, and make the surviving examples more like the Clydesdale, perhaps less compact and robust than their ancestors.

The Clydesdale

The Clydesdale is the draught horse of Scotland and the Border country, although equally at home in Ulster and the north of England. Until recent years it was also exported in great numbers to Australia and New Zealand, where there were numerous settlers of Scottish ancestry. It is slightly smaller than the Shire with less bulk but perhaps more spirit and speed, having comparatively longer legs. Descended from native mares breeding with imported Flemish stallions, Clydesdales were first recognised as a separate breed during the late eighteenth century, although a breed society was not founded until 1877. Although originally reared and bred for farmwork in Clydesdale or Lanarkshire (Strathclyde) they were also popular from the early days for street work in the mining and industrial areas of central Scotland. They worked in large teams for the shipyards and foundries and were noted for their smart, brisk action, much quicker than that of the Shire, but they were of less reliable temperament. They were usually bays, browns and blacks although most horses had some white markings, especially on face, nose and legs.

The Suffolk Punch

The Suffolk Punch was a chestnut horse, often with a much lighter mane and tail, bred mainly in East Anglia. It was seldom more than 16 hands (1.63 metres) high, with a deep body and comparatively short legs. Its ancestry is as distinguished as that of the Shire breed, traced back to the middle ages, although with great improvements from the eighteenth century onwards. The word *punch* means rotund yet firm and compact and seems to express its character even more than the conformation of the animal. Although mainly an agricultural horse it was also in demand for heavy cartage work, especially in the London area and south-east England, and for breeding weight-carrying hunters. It could pull a heavy load at the trot and was once used by the Reverend Sir John Cullham — a great admirer of the breed — to draw his private coach on a tour of Clwyd in North Wales, over rough roads and stiff gradients that might have defeated other breeds. The Suffolk Punch is almost clean-legged, with very little feather or long hair on the pasterns. It thrives well on very little food, being remarkable for health and longevity. One Suffolk mare produced a healthy prizewinning foal at the age of thirty-seven, at least ten years in advance of the life span of most working horses. Like the Shire it is normally good-tempered and easy to handle.

The Percheron

The Percheron is of French descent and was introduced into Britain during and shortly after the First World War, having greatly impressed both the War Department and many farmers serving in the British Expeditionary Force with its courage and endurance as an artillery horse. The stallion is about 16 hands 3 inches (1.70 metres), while the mare is about 2 inches (50 millimetres) shorter. This makes it midway in height between the Shire and the Suffolk. It is either grey or black, especially in England, although a few brown and chestnut horses are seen in France, frowned upon by the English breed society. They are excellent workers with clean, hard limbs and an appearance of great dignity. They combine the briskness of the Clydesdale and hardness of the Suffolk with the docility and willingness of the Shire. As an all-round worker the Percheron (named after a district in France) is spirited yet strong and untiring, temperament alone making it ideal for the novice to handle. During the nineteenth century large numbers were exported to the United States and Canada, while in recent years they have found unexpected favour on small farms in Japan.

Other farm horses

The above were all horses of pure breed and distinguished ancestry, which only the more prosperous farmers could afford. On many farms and holdings most of the working horses were crossbred and better described as Shire or Clydesdale types. This need not detract from their sterling qualities, especially as there were many jobs about the farm for which great size and strength were scarcely necessary or even desirable. When extra strength was needed on a heavy machine or wagon the farmer's riding cob (the cob was a dual-purpose riding and light draught horse) or his son's medium-weight hunter might be hitched alongside larger and more powerful carthorses. Up to the 1940s many farmers, especially in Yorkshire and the midlands, bred horses for town work, especially for brewers, haulage contractors and the railway cartage services. Before the Second World War large numbers of army horses were bred on farms for artillery, pack and general draught purposes.

On the hill farms of Britain Welsh cobs, standard cobs, Fell and Dale ponies were widely used. Most of these could be ridden, driven or used as pack animals, being extremely versatile and handy, especially where there were few good roads. In the Highlands and islands of Scotland the Highland pony or garron was a useful animal, able to graze and survive where sheep, goats and red deer would have difficulty in finding a living. Even the tiny Shetland was originally used in agriculture, mainly as a pack animal in the peat bogs.

Cart harness

The main type of harness for draught horses on the farm was cart harness, chain or sling gear and plough gear. Cart harness was the type used for drawing carts, wagons and implements with

Fig. 48. Cart harness.

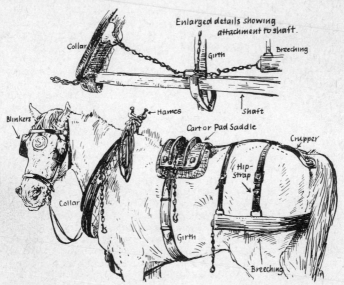

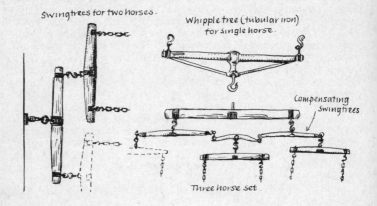

Swingtrees for two horses.

Whipple tree (tubular iron) for single horse.

Compensating Swingtrees

Three horse set.

Fig. 49. Swing and whippletrees for draught.

shafts, either single or double. It was mainly used with a single horse or the shaft horse of a team of several in tandem. Shafts or thills were straight or curved poles on either side of the horse, attached to the vehicle or implement at one end and to harness fittings of the draught gear at the other. Curved shafts were mainly used when the centre of gravity was low and the vehicle or implement near the ground, especially those on cranked axles with heavy loads or tare weights. On some shafts there were underprops or propsticks to help support the vehicle and its load when at rest. Double shafts, especially on wagons, were mainly used in the eastern counties and required extra space or breadth when passing through gateways and barn doors. When more than one horse was needed they were more frequently placed one behind the other, with chain traces leading back to the wagon shafts or to attachments on the harness of the horse just behind. Alternatively stretchers, whippletrees, swingletrees or spreaders — made of wood or iron — were used as explained in the diagram above.

The main part of harness was the draught collar, which was put on the horse first, even before the bridle. It was normally put on upside down and turned at the base of the neck. The heavy draught collar had metal hames or curved bars sunk into depressions at the front of the collar, which was made of leather and cloth well padded with straw and flock on the underside. Attachments on the collar were hooks and mountings for tug chains leading to the shafts and for rein rings or territs. A good collar was the work of a specialist craftsman and had to be a perfect fit to avoid neck galls and sores. Neck collars were worn on most farms as they suited the build and conformation of the average British draught horse with high shoulders, far better than the lighter breast harness of some continental countries. A neck collar and bridle were worn with all types of gear. Straps connecting the hames at the top were known as the toplatch. They were connected at the bottom of the collar by links and hooks. A few hames were also attached at the top with chain links rather than straps.

The carthorse bridle consisted of several fairly broad, heavy straps, being the noseband, browband, cheek straps and throat lash. A vee strap (or V strap) was fastened on top of the head with leads to the blinkers, or protective eye shades worn by most draught horses to prevent them catching a glimpse of the following vehicle or implement, which was known to unnerve a young or badly broken animal. The eye of the horse enables it to see both forwards and backwards without turning its head very far in either direction.

The cart pad or saddle rested in the centre or slight hollow of the back, between loins and withers or shoulders. It was well

Fig. 50. Chain harness or trace gear.

padded, like the collar, and had upper grooves through which a chain or ridger could be passed that linked with iron loops on the shafts, both right and left. While the pad was secured on the underside with a girth or bellyband, it was prevented from slipping forwards or backwards by the use of crupper and meeter straps. The crupper fitted with a loop round the tail and was not always worn by heavy horses. Vertical hip and loin straps on the hindquarters supported a breeching band or web that helped the horse when backing or to hold its load back on a steep slope. A strap between collar and girth, passing between the forelegs and often loaded with ornamental brasses, was the martingale.

Chain harness and plough gear

Chain harness was used for drawing implements such as ploughs and harrows and usually lacked cart pad and breeching web. A similar type of gear was also used when two horses were hitched as a pair to either side of a draught pole, which might be found on mowing machines, large seed drills and certain types of wagon. Chain traces or harness led directly back to a stretcher bar or whippletree, hooked at the front or splinter bar of the item to be

Fig. 51. Plough harness.

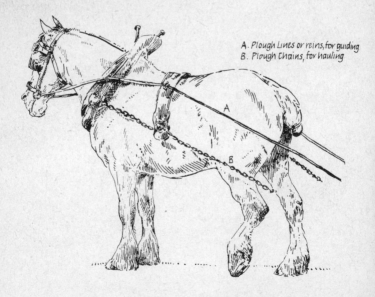

A. Plough Lines or reins, for guiding
B. Plough Chains, for hauling

drawn. There would also be, in these circumstances, a neck strap to support the front end of the pole, missing in plough gear. Trace harness, worn by two or more horses in tandem, was in the form of chains leading back to the shafts or whippletree, as previously explained. Whippletrees were either wood, steel or tubular iron, the wooden type having iron or steel mountings. Horses working side by side or as a pair were usually attached to each other by leather straps between their bridles and often to wooden bars at the head of the pole. Using plough, trace and chain harness was always known as 'working in chains'.

Horse brasses

Most cart and plough horses on the farm wore decorative horse brasses both on bridles and on the straps of body harness. These were made of solid brass and burnished by the horsemen, carters or ploughmen to shine like silver. They are said to be of prehistoric and pagan origin, worn by all draught animals and beasts of burden to ward off the evil eye and bring good luck to the harvest. Some horses, especially wagon teams, also wore bells or swingers on their harness and bridles. These helped to serve as a warning of their approach when working on the road, especially near corners or crossings. Although early brasses were simple cross, shield or crescent shapes, some of those produced during the mid nineteenth century were more imaginative, in the form of prancing horses, rampant lions, running foxes, windmills and even railway locomotives. Many modern brasses are cheap imitations, not always of brass.

11. Inventors and manufacturers

The great agricultural revolution of the eighteenth century was just as important as the industrial revolution which began during the same century. Both were significant stages in the development of modern civilisation, predominantly influenced by the contributions of British inventors, theorists and pioneers. The Scots and English may be said to have been both the prophets and practitioners of this movement although it was often left to the Americans and other nationalities to perfect ideas that were slow to spread in their country of origin. While England was always comparatively advanced in farming methods, renowned for the production of grain and later wool throughout the known world, Scotland — with a smaller population and less fertile land area — was far more backward than most European countries until the mid eighteenth century. Yet from the second half of the century the agricultural skill and economy of Scotland, especially in the lowlands, increased beyond all recognition. At one period Scottish farmers were constantly moving south to buy up the holdings of less thrifty Englishmen and teach their neighbours more than a few lessons in agriculture. James Small and his compatriot Wilkie were renowned throughout western Europe for their contributions to ploughing and cultivation. Andrew Meikle invented the first practical threshing machine, while Finlayson developed the forerunner of the cultivator and the Reverend Patrick Bell made one of the greatest contributions of all time with his mechanical reaper. Britain certainly had her store of genius in this sphere, although hampered by the conservative attitude of all classes and by the failure of those with money and influence to provide the necessary backing.

Younger countries such as the United States, Canada and Australia were more eager and willing to take risks both with their own ideas and with the inventions or methods of other nations. Yet the McCormick empire of Chicago and the Massey-Harris empire of Toronto were by no means unchallenged. The leading British firms such as Ransomes of Ipswich were able to hold their own at least from the second half of the nineteenth century and at one period nearly all the large towns in agricultural districts, from Shrewsbury to Gloucester and Colchester to Lincoln, were centres for the making and marketing of farm machinery, although perhaps not so much as the Americans in the international sphere.

Trade and commercial enterprise have never been as respectable in Britain as with some of her greatest rivals, and the wealth and diversity of British inventive genius has rarely been matched by business acumen or astute salesmanship.

A remarkable feature of the agricultural revolution and era of land improvement was the diversity of backgrounds and occupations from which the pioneers and inventors were drawn. While some were farmers and country craftsmen, many came from walks of life not even remotely connected with agriculture. Jethro Tull was a barrister and amateur organist, turned farmer by way of diversion; Patrick Bell was an ordained clergyman while Henry Ogle was a schoolmaster. Even members of the landed aristocracy made their contribution; the second Earl of Ducie, during the mid nineteenth century, devoted much of his time to farming improvements, not only inventing a cultivator named after him but setting up his own works at Uley, Gloucestershire, for the manufacture of farm machinery.

The first machines and implements were assembled by village craftsmen, often being the combined work of blacksmith, wheelwright and joiner or carpenter. Others made their contribution after serving an apprenticeship under such craftsmen or at the small forges and foundries which were found even in remote rural areas until the nineteenth century. Robert Ransome, the son of a Quaker schoolmaster and inventor of the revolutionary self-sharpening plough, was apprenticed to an ironmonger in Norwich, although he later entered business with one of the first iron and brass foundries of any size in East Anglia. He patented his method for tempering ploughshares in 1785 but later moved to Ipswich, which was then a thriving port in the overseas and coastal trade, nearer to London and a far better centre than Norwich then was for trading by land and sea. It may be remembered that Mc-Cormick set up a great factory in Chicago, because it was in a central position both for the wheat belts of America and for transport by land and water to all parts of that continent and eventually the world. Ransomes of Ipswich eventually became the largest British manufacturer of farm implements but later produced such diverse items as steam pumps for industry, traction engines and even trolley buses. Another entrepreneur in this field was Frederick Savage of King's Lynn, who was born at Hevingham in Norfolk and served as apprentice to a whitesmith and machine maker of East Dereham. He is perhaps better known for his patent fairground machinery and equipment exported to all parts of the English-speaking world, although his fortunes and the success of the St Nicholas Works at King's Lynn were based on the supply and repair of horse-drawn farm implements. He was a man of great personal enterprise and imagination and the Savage empire soon crumbled after his death, his brothers being unable to cope for more than a few years. The present firm is no longer a family business although it still bears his name. At one period Savage concerned himself with improving the two-wheeled cart or tumbril as a general-purpose farm vehicle. He also improved the elevator for stackyards, his version having enlarged prongs or tines on a double web. At a later stage he combined with a fellow inventor named Goss to produce the Goss-Savage patent horse hoe. This was a two-wheeled hoe of cast iron throughout, having a vast number and variety of tines or feet for digging out weeds.

Many large and small firms making agricultural machinery began as country forges; these included such well known names as Garretts of Leiston and Burrells of Thetford — both eventually noted for their road traction engines used by farmers and travelling showmen. They frequently diversified their businesses to making a wide range of products only distantly connected with farming but owed their greatest prosperity to the manufacture of agricultural tools and horse-drawn implements.

12. Where to see horse-drawn farm machinery

Dates and hours of opening vary and readers are advised to check them before making a special journey.

ENGLAND

BERKSHIRE
Museum of English Rural Life, University of Reading, Whiteknights Park, Reading. Telephone: Reading (0734) 85123 extension 475. A permanent collection of implements and farm tools, including ploughs, drills, reapers, hoes and a wide range of typical farm wagons.

CAMBRIDGESHIRE
Farmland Museum, 50 High Street, Haddenham, Ely. Telephone: Ely (0353) 740381. A private collection mainly concerning the agriculture of the Fens.

Wimpole Home Farm, Arrington, near Royston. Telephone: Cambridge (0223) 208987. Fine collection of machinery, vehicles and implements in NT estate home attached to Wimpole Hall.

CLEVELAND
Newham Grange Leisure Farm, Coulby Newham, Middlesbrough. Telephone: Middlesbrough (0642) 36762. Displays of farming equipment.

CORNWALL
North Cornwall Museum and Gallery, The Clease, Camelford. Exhibits include wagons, carts and farm machinery.

DERBYSHIRE
Elvaston Working Estate Museum, Borrowash Road, Elvaston, near Derby. Telephone: Derby (0332) 73799. Displays of horse-drawn implements and farm vehicles in an estate farm.

DEVON
Alscott Farm Museum, Shebbear. Telephone: Shebbear (040 928) 206. Several horse ploughs and other early implements.

Ashley Countryside Collection, Ashley House, Wembworthy, Chulmleigh. Telephone: Ashreigney (076 93) 226. Contains twelve different types of plough.

Furze Farm Park, Bridgerule, Holsworthy. Telephone Bridgerule (028 881) 342. Implements, tools and equipment, with demonstrations of old-time harvesting and threshing in season.

James Countryside Museum, Bicton Gardens, East Budleigh. Telephone: Budleigh Salterton (039 54) 3881. Several farm implements and a number of carts, trucks and wagons.

Steam and Countryside Museum, Sandy Bay, Exmouth. Telephone: Exmouth (039 52) 74533. Ploughs, harrows, seed drills, sail reaper, threshers, hay sweep.

Tiverton Museum, St Andrew's Street, Tiverton. Telephone: Tiverton (0884) 256295. Farm machinery and equipment, including a rare harrow from Norway.

DURHAM
North of England Open Air Museum, Beamish Hall, Stanley. Telephone: Stanley (0207) 31811. Collection of farm carts and early implements, among many other things of local interest.

EAST SUSSEX
Drusillas, Berwick. Telephone: Alfriston (0323) 870234. Primarily a centre for rare breeds, also exhibiting farm implements, old wagons and ox harness.

Michelham Priory, Upper Dicker, near Hailsham. Telephone: Hailsham (0323) 844224. Collection of wagons and horse ploughs.

Wilmington Priory Agricultural Museum, Wilmington, Polegate. Telephone: Alfriston (0323) 870537. The agricultural collection of the Sussex Archaeological Society.

GLOUCESTERSHIRE
Cotswold Countryside Collection, Northleach. Telephone: Northleach (045 16) 715. Many vehicles and items of equipment.

Folk Museum, 99-103 Westgate, Gloucester. Telephone: Gloucester (0452) 26467. Exhibits include farm tools and an early seed drill made by a local firm.

Smerrill Farm Museum, Kemble, near Cirencester. Telephone: Kemble (028 577) 208. The Clement Collection of agricultural items from the horse era is displayed in a Cotswold barn.

GREATER LONDON
Science Museum, Exhibition Road, South Kensington, London. Telephone: 01-598 6371. Numerous implements of all types, illustrating the history of farming.

Upminster Tithe Barn Agricultural and Folk Museum, Hall Lane, Upminster. Telephone: Upminster (040 22) 29614. The collection includes a seed drill, scarifier, two Ransomes ploughs, an example of horse gear and a number of swingletrees.

GREATER MANCHESTER
Rochdale Museum, Sparrow Hill, Rochdale. Telephone: Rochdale (0706) 47474 extension 769. There is a collection of implements used on local farms.

HAMPSHIRE
Breamore Countryside Museum, Breamore House, Fordingbridge. Telephone: Breamore (072 57) 233. Collections of hand tools, horse- and ox-drawn implements.

HEREFORD AND WORCESTER
Almonry Museum, Vine Street, Evesham. Telephone: Evesham (0386) 6944. Mainly agricultural and market-gardening machinery from the Vale of Evesham.

Bewdley Museum, The Shambles, Load Street, Bewdley. Telephone: Bewdley (0299) 403573. A small collection of farm implements, including threshing box, seed drill, reaper binder and horse plough.

HERTFORDSHIRE
St Albans City Museum, Hatfield Road, St Albans. Telephone: St Albans (0727) 56679. A small collection of horse-drawn implements and vehicles, but the largest collection of craft tools in the country.

ISLE OF WIGHT
Yafford Mill, Shorwell. Telephone: Brighstone (0983) 740610. An old watermill with a collection of farm implements and horse-drawn vehicles.

KENT
Wye College Agricultural Museum, Brook, near Ashford. Telephone: Ashford (0233) 812401. Agricultural implements and horse-drawn vehicles, many connected with local hop farming.

LEICESTERSHIRE
Rutland County Museum, Catmos Street, Oakham. Telephone: Oakham (0572) 3654. Collection of ploughs, wagons and farm implements used in Leicestershire and Rutland.

LINCOLNSHIRE
Church Farm Museum, Church Road South, Skegness. Telephone: Skegness (0754) 66658. The Bernard Best Collection of agricultural and domestic equipment.

Mawthorpe Collection of Bygones, Woodlands, Mawthorpe, Alford. Telephone: Alford (052 12) 2336. Early farm implements and wagons.

Museum of Lincolnshire Life, Burton Road, Lincoln. Telephone: Lincoln (0522) 28448. Many early horse-drawn machines, tools and items of equipment. There are also threshing boxes and a number of early carts and wagons.

NORFOLK
Church Farm, Martham, Great Yarmouth. Telephone: Great Yarmouth (0493) 740223. Numerous early implements with demonstrations of their use with heavy horses.

Norfolk Rural Life Museum, Beech House, Gressenhall, East Dereham. Telephone: Dereham (0362) 860563. An interesting selection of early farm tools and horse-drawn equipment.

NORTH YORKSHIRE
Ryedale Folk Museum, Hutton-le-Hole. Telephone: Lastingham (075 15) 367. Agricultural implements and wagons.

Yorkshire Museum of Farming, Murton Park, York. Telephone York (0904) 489731.

OXFORDSHIRE
Cogges Agricultural Heritage Museum, Cogges, Witney. Telephone: Witney (0993) 72602. Equipment in a traditional farm setting.

SHROPSHIRE
Acton Scott, Wenlock Edge, Acton Scott, Church Stretton. Telephone: Marshbrook (069 46) 306. A working farm, with displays and exhibits of early farm implements. Frequent demonstrations of the larger items.

The White House Country Life Museum, Aston Munslow. Telephone: Munslow (058 476) 661. A traditional farm with numerous implements and horse-drawn vehicles.

SOMERSET
Somerset Rural Life Museum, Abbey Farm, Chilkwell Street, Glastonbury. Telephone: Glastonbury (0458) 32903. Horse-drawn implements, vehicles and equipment of all types.

STAFFORDSHIRE
Staffordshire County Museum, Shugborough, Stafford. Telephone: Little Haywood (0889) 881388. The home farm is now a farm museum with numerous horse-drawn implements, especially ploughs, harrows and cultivators.

SUFFOLK
Easton Farm Park, Model Farm, Easton, Woodbridge. Telephone: Wickham Market (0728) 746475. Suffolk horses are used to demonstrate implements in the collection.

Museum of East Anglian Life, Stowmarket. Telephone: Stowmarket (044 92) 2229. Horse-drawn vehicles and implements, displayed in a medieval barn.

SURREY
Old Kiln Museum, Reeds Road, Tilford, Farnham. Telephone: Frensham (025 125) 2300. The Jackson Collection of horse-drawn implements, including a horse-geared elevator and many farm vehicles.

WARWICKSHIRE
Mary Arden's House, Wilmcote. Telephone: Stratford-upon-Avon (0789) 3455. A collection of old Warwickshire farm implements and equipment, carts and wagons.

WEST YORKSHIRE
Grammar School Museum, Heptonstall, near Hebden Bridge. Telephone enquiries: Halifax (0422) 54823. A collection of local implements and equipment, also photographic records and references.

Ryburn Farm Museum, Ripponden. Telephone: Halifax (0422) 54823. Equipment used on north Pennine farms.

West Yorkshire Folk Museum, Shibden Hall, Halifax. Telephone: Halifax (0422) 52246. Several horse-drawn implements and items of early farming equipment.

ISLE OF MAN

Manx Museum, Douglas. Telephone: Douglas (0624) 5522. Several agricultural implements on display.

NORTHERN IRELAND

Ardress Farmyard Museum, Annaghmore, County Down. Telephone: Annaghmore (0762) 1236. Farming equipment from last 150 years.

Ulster Folk and Transport Museum, Cultra Manor, Holywood, County Down. Telephone: Holywood (023 17) 5411. An extensive collection of early horse-drawn implements as used in Northern Ireland.

SCOTLAND

GRAMPIAN
Adamston Agricultural Museum, Huntly, Aberdeenshire. Telephone: Drumblade (0466) 231. Horse and hand implements as used in the north-east of Scotland.

STRATHCLYDE
Argyll Museum of Farming Life, Auchindrain, Inveraray, Argyll. Telephone: Furnace (049 95) 235. A deserted farm village now restored with implements and hand tools.

TAYSIDE
Angus Folk Museum, Kirkwynd, Glamis, Angus. The collection includes agricultural machines and items, many connected with the Reverend Patrick Bell, inventor of the reaping machine.

WALES

DYFED
Scolton Manor Museum, Spittal, Haverfordwest. Telephone: Clarbeston (043 782) 328. Many pieces of horse-drawn equipment.

GWENT
Rural Crafts Museum, Monmouth Street, Usk. Telephone: Usk (029 13) 2394. Agricultural tools and bygones.

POWYS
Brecknock Museum, Brecon. Telephone: Brecon (0874) 4121. The collection includes numerous items of agricultural equipment.

SOUTH GLAMORGAN

Welsh Folk Museum, St Fagans. Telephone: Cardiff (0222) 569441. Many horse-drawn vehicles and implements connected with farming in Wales.

Glossary

Barn machinery: a fixed rather than portable machine, such as a chaff cutter, kept in a barn.

Bell crank: lever with two arms, having a common fulcrum at their place of joining.

Binder: reaping machine that both cuts and binds corn in sheaves. Also known as a reaper binder or string binder. Early types used wire but later types used string or twine.

Box seat: high front seat on certain horse-drawn vehicles and implements. Originally a box containing valuables, on which the driver sat to ensure their safety. Later a tool box.

Broadcast: sow seed or distribute manure in a random manner. Seed was often sown in this way by hand, the sower flinging handfuls alternately left and right as he walked the furrows. Box-type machines and seed fiddles were later introduced.

Cart gear: harness for a carthorse with pad saddle and breeching, as used in drawing a cart or wagon.

Cart lodge: shed, usually thatched, in a farmyard or the corner of a field, where a cart or implement may be kept. Open-sided but with enough cover to keep off the worst of wind and rain.

Chain horse: extra horse working in chains or chain harness, preceding a shaft horse in tandem.

Chains: chain traces used by chain horses.

Combine: combine harvester that replaced the reaper binder during the twentieth century, although not widely used in Britain until the 1940s. Early types were drawn by about forty horses per hitch. It cut and threshed in one action.

Coulter: vertical cutting knife mounted on the front of a plough. This opened the way for the horizontal slice of the share.

Coulter tube: combined tube and coulter on a seed drill.

Cultivator: machine used in breaking up the sods of a ploughed field. Form of harrow on wheels, the tines or teeth fixed to bars behind rear travelling wheels. Each tine may be adjusted individually.

Digging stick: primitive hand tool used like a pickaxe or mattock, later replaced by the plough.

Draught pole: used on certain horse-drawn vehicles and implements. An attachment between draught animals and the load they hauled. Horses were hitched in pairs on either side of a pole.

Drill: machine invented or perfected by Jethro Tull about 1702. Used for sowing in neat drills or rows as opposed to the wasteful method of broadcasting.

Drills: long neat rows, depressed by the foot of a coulter tube on a drill, used for drilling or machine sowing.

Elevator: stackyard machine of a portable type used for the mechanical stacking of hay and corn sheaves.

Feather: fetlocks or long hairs on the lower limbs of a carthorse, especially a Shire horse.

Finger bar: slotted bar in which the fingers or cutting blades of a mower slide from side to side in cutting the crop.

Fingers: the flattened, wedge-shaped knife blades of a mowing or reaping machine.

Grubber: type of cultivator, the tines of which were mainly in advance of the rear wheels. Adjusted by vertical lift of the whole machine.

Hake: notched vertical loop, for draught purposes, at the front of a plough. Attached to the frame by means of a horizontal quadrant.

Harrow: flat machine or press with teeth or spikes on the underside. Used in breaking up the clods of ploughland or covering the seedbed after sowing.

Hay lifter: elevator towed behind a hay cart, used in raising hay from the windrows to the loading platform. This cut out much of the heavy manual work with a pitchfork.

Hay sledge: a small flat cart or wheel-less vehicle used in collecting hay on mountains and moorland farms. A larger vehicle with wheels might overturn on steep slopes.

Hay sweep: appliance with long wooden bars, tipped with iron or steel, for gathering up hay from the swaths with a scooping motion.

Hitch: the means of securing a horse or other beast of burden to its load.

Horse fork: simple pulley-lift with a grab device, for lifting hay from wagon to rick. Operated by a draught horse walking backwards and forwards. Replaced by the elevator.

Knife bar: the same as a finger bar, supporting the blades of a mower or reaper.

Ladders: detachable ladder-like structures at either end of a vehicle to help support an overhanging load.

Land cap: metal bar on the side of a plough to keep it steady and hold back the soil above the furrow.

Land wheels: the wheels of a farm implement supporting it during work on the land. On a plough the smaller of two front wheels supporting the weight of the machine on the landward side away from the furrow.

Mouldboard: part of a plough that lays or turns back the furrow, directly behind the share. Either all metal or metal-sheathed. Its height and shape decide the form and angle of the furrow.

Pastern: joint above a horse's hoof between hoof and leg. With a Shire or Clydesdale this part is covered in thick long hair or feather.

Pawls: the raised part of gears on machines and implements, working against a small lever or ratchet. These are responsible for the clicking noise of mowers and reapers.

Pitching: raising hay or sheaves of corn on to rick or cart by means of pitchforks.

Plough gear: the trace harness of a plough horse without cart pad or breeching.

Plow: old English spelling of plough, still used in the United States of America.

Pole: same as draught pole.

Pyke: a small rick or haycock.

Rick lifter: low cart on to which haycocks may be winched for transport. Used mainly in Scotland and the north of England.

Riding machine: machine or implement with a seat for the driver, usually found on heavier and more modern types of equipment than the old-style walking machine.

Rig: any type of machine or vehicle. Also a collective noun for horses, vehicle and harness.

Semi-grubber: type of grubber with the bars or tines both in front and behind the main land wheels. Between a grubber and a cultivator.

Shaft horse: also known as a wheeler or thill horse. Works next to the load with a team or tandem pair.

Share: the pointed and wedge-shaped fitment of a plough, between coulter and mouldboard. This is responsible for the horizontal slice.

Side-delivery rake: form of rake in which the prongs, in three rows, are mounted diagonally and sideways, throwing out or turning the hay with a sideways movement.

Slade: plough accessory or fitment running in the sole or bottom of the furrow, to balance the plough.

Stalk: extension often used with a bracket to support a small land wheel on a farm implement.

Steersman: driver in control of a farm machine or of its steering device. Not always in charge of the horses.

Stilts: the handles and handgrips of a horse plough.

Stook: several sheaves of corn stacked together, round central air space, for drying.

Stripper: combine harvester stripping off the ears of wheat but ignoring the standing straw. Widely used in Australia and North America.

Swath turner: machine with sideways revolving tines used in turning the hay. Less complex than the side-delivery rake.

Swing plough: wooden beamed plough without wheels.

Tampcock: small haycock or stack.

Tedder: originally a tidder or tidding machine. Box-like machine with revolving tines, used for turning the hay in a backwards direction.

Threshing box: name usually given to a box-like portable threshing machine. Little used since the coming of the combine and stripper.

Tines: straight or curved bars or teeth used with a variety of implements. Similar to the prongs of a fork.

Trackage: marks or furrows left by the land wheels of a heavy machine.

Turnwrest: plough widely used on downland farms in the south of England. The direction of furrow slice could be changed at the end of each row to effect up and down rather than continuous ploughing. This was done by making adjustments on the plough rather than by turning the implement.

Walking machine: a machine controlled by a driver or steersman plodding on foot at the side or rear. Not a riding machine.

Whippletree: horizontal bar or bow shape to which the traces of a draught horse may be attached for certain types of gear. Mainly used with a draught pole.

Windrow: drying hay in long neat rows from which it might be either collected directly or made into haycocks.

Bibliography

Bond, J. R. *Farm Implements and Machinery.* Benn, 1923.

Clarke, Ronald. *Savages Limited: A Short History.* Newcomen Society, 1967.

Grace, D. R. and Philips, D. C. *Ransomes of Ipswich.* Institute of Agricultural History, 1975.

Huggett, Frank. *Farming.* A. & C. Black, 1963.

James and Burn. *Farm Implements and Machines* (ed. H. Stephens). Blackwood, 1858.

Keegan, Terry. *The Heavy Horse: Its Harness and Harness Decoration.* Pelham Books, 1973.

Partridge, Michael. *Early Farm Machinery.* Hugh Evelyn, 1969.

Ransome, James Allen. *The Implements of Agriculture.* J. Ridgeway, 1843.

Stephens, H. *Jethro Tull: His Influence on Mechanised Agriculture.* Blackwood, 1958.

Thompson, John. *Horse-drawn Farm Implements, Parts I, II and III.* John Thompson, 1978.

Toulson, Shirley. *Discovering Farm Museums and Farm Parks.* Shire Publications, 1977.

Vince, John. *Vintage Farm Machines.* Shire Publications, second edition 1978.

Wright, Philip A. *Old Farm Implements.* David and Charles, 1974.

Wright, Philip A. *Salute the Carthorse.* Ian Allan, 1971.

Index